PREPARING
FOR
BATTLE

LEARN THE SECRETS TO TOP SPIRITUAL WARFARE

PREPARING
FOR
BATTLE

PAMELA BRABOY JACKSON
J. J. WILKINS, JR.

SYNERGY Publishers
Gainesville, Florida 32614 USA

A division of Bridge-Logos International Trust
in partnership with **Bridge-Logos** *Publishers*

Preparing for Battle
by Pamela Braboy Jackson and J. J. Wilkins, Jr.
© 2002 by Pamela Braboy Jackson and J. J. Wilkins, Jr.
All rights reserved

www.preparing4battle.com

International Standard Book Number: 1-931727-09-0
Library of Congress Catalog Card Number: 2002111611

Published by:
Synergy Publishers
Gainesville, Florida 32614 USA

Synergy Publishers is a division of Bridge-Logos International Trust, Inc., a not-for-profit corporation, in partnership with Bridge-Logos Publishers.

DEDICATION

We dedicate this book to our
loving and supportive families.

This book is also dedicated to the special memory
of Harriett "Hattie" Burnett Doggert.

CONTENTS

ACKNOWLEDGMENTS

We would like to acknowledge our Wake Chapel Church (WCC) family of Raleigh, North Carolina and our new sister church, Sherwood Oaks Christian Church (SOCC) of Bloomington, Indiana. It is through the continued quest for spiritual growth that we are able to identify those areas of Christian life that seem to need more direct clarification. The nurturance we feel from our communities of faith cannot go without recognition.

We thank God for these inspired words through His Holy Spirit. His message to you is to be encouraged. Remember, the battle is not yours; it is the Lord's.

INTRODUCTION

WHAT & WHY?

In the midst of private storms and personal tragedies in life, have you ever asked yourself, "What is going on? Why is this happening to me?" Many people have asked God these questions time and time again. The circumstances in your life are not random occurrences. *Preparing for Battle* explains to you the "what and why" in your life. Before beginning, however, you must believe you're a winner! We pray you will be inspired and encouraged, knowing "We are more than conquerors through him that loved us" (Romans 8:37). ✗

Spiritual warfare is not a new topic. It has been described by prophets, discussed by theologians and debated by scholars for centuries. The Bible is full of the language of warfare. Even if you are the type of person who does not feel comfortable with warfare language, you must learn about spiritual warfare in order to be a stronger witness for our Lord and Savior, Jesus Christ. The most elaborate description of spiritual warfare can be found in the sixth chapter of the book of Ephesians. It reads:

> Put on the whole armour of God, that ye may be able to stand against the wiles of the devil. For we wrestle not against flesh and blood, but against principalities, against powers, against the rulers of the darkness of this world, against spiritual wickedness in high places. Wherefore take unto you the whole armour of God, that ye may be able to withstand in the evil day, and having done all, to stand. Stand therefore, having your loins girt about with truth, and having on the breastplate of

righteousness; And your feet shod with the preparation of the gospel of peace; Above all, taking the shield of faith, wherewith ye shall be able to quench all the fiery darts of the wicked. And take the helmet of salvation, and the sword of the Spirit, which is the word of God: Praying always with all prayer and supplication in the Spirit, and watching thereunto with all perseverance and supplication for all saints (Ephesians 6:11–18).

Notice that Paul is speaking to the church. Spiritual warfare is an ongoing battle faced by Christians. You can be involved in a spiritual battle and not know it. We will point out subtle ways the enemy can attack your life as well as obvious traps that are set for Christians.

> **Spiritual warfare is an ongoing battle faced by Christians.**

The secret to spiritual warfare is to focus on the outcome—you are the winner! If you keep this in mind, you can conquer all of the demons that attack your life. In order to be victorious, however, you must understand how to fight the battle.

Purpose

The purpose of this book is to serve as a resource for those enlisted in the Army of Our Lord and Savior, Jesus Christ. It is a road map for those who are new to the Christian faith, pointing out what you can expect on this faith walk. For the more "mature" Christian, this book will allow you to evaluate your walk with Christ. Are you still growing or have you hit a brick wall, spiritually? We will explain why you may not be growing as quickly as you expected. For those of you who have been a part of the church for most of your lives (the veteran Christian), this book will serve as a check and balance sheet. It will also help identify life experiences that you can use to encourage other Christians.

Preparing for Battle challenges every Christian to discover the hidden secrets of spiritual warfare. We pray you will read this entire book for it includes truths that Satan does not want you to know. It is a wake-up call. We're sounding the alarm. You would not believe the number of times the computer "crashed" while putting this project together—more than chance alone could explain! Technical problems simply provide confirmation of the importance of dispensing knowledge of our walk with Christ. The Bible tells us God's people perish for lack of knowledge (Hosea 4:6). This book provides a very simple description of the meaning of spiritual warfare and how it is related to the everyday problems faced by Christians.

History

We are often born into a religious dogma. Because our parents were raised as Christians, we consider ourselves Christians. Approximately 80% of Americans inherit their religious affiliation from their ancestors. Although this is a common phenomenon around the world, the problem is many of us do not seek God for ourselves. Instead, we rely on the prayers of others to carry us through our difficult moments. We never really make the connection between the confession we made with our mouths that Christ Jesus is Lord and the subsequent problems we have in our lives.

When you announced to your church family that you believed in Christ Jesus, you took sides in a *war*. You chose Jesus and rejected Satan. Your name was scratched from Satan's list of supporters and placed on his most wanted list. Now, let us describe to you the rules of engagement and how this battle will advance.

CHAPTER 1

RULES OF ENGAGEMENT

*For it is better, if the will of God be so, that ye
suffer for well doing, than for evil doing.*
—1 Peter 3:17

Good things happen to good people and bad things
happen to bad people, right? If you look at the people
around you or those in the news, you know this isn't true.
At times, we can expect to face struggles, especially when
it's time for us to grow spiritually. Problems are always
opportunities for growth. The biblical story of Job, in
addition to countless scriptures, reminds us God is
sovereign and every good gift comes from God.

How This Thing Works

Your mission is to advance the kingdom of God on
earth. You have joined a long and sustained campaign to
defeat the enemy—to break through enemy lines and take
back what the devil has stolen from you and mankind.
What has he stolen? He stole health, prosperity, world
peace and the simple lives of your family members and

friends. It has always been God's will that mankind be fruitful and multiply. Satan is trying to divert God's plan; he comes to kill, steal and destroy (John 10:10).

As a soldier, you must proceed to the front lines of the conflict and prepare to fight the battles that confront you. You have been called to spread the good news of our resurrected Christ. You have been commissioned to tell a dying world that Jesus died that the world might have life more abundantly. It is your job to let the downtrodden know that even if Jesus has to reach way down, He will pick you up.

Our God is a God of low places. He will help you when you feel like you're in a low valley. Always remember God has given you the final victory. "No weapon that is formed against thee shall prosper" (Isaiah 54:17).

The way you begin this task is by invoking and demonstrating the love of God in all you say and do. Love is the key. To make it plain and simple, you must spread love throughout the land. Demonstrate love and compassion to others that they may glorify your Father which is in heaven.

This can be a hard assignment because we are born into societies that embrace certain prejudices and biases toward other people. Instead of questioning why we react in particular ways when confronted by those unlike ourselves, we go through our daily lives pretending these are natural responses. Did you know that social psychologists have discovered a way for us to discard our stereotypes? They have found that when we learn personal information about a person, we start treating that person as a unique individual rather than a member of a stigmatized group.

The enemy uses many distractions and prejudice is one of them. Prepare your mind to share the good news of Jesus Christ to all who are willing to listen—regardless of age, creed, ethnicity or gender. Godlike love (agape) has no boundaries. "This is my commandment, that ye love one another, as I have loved you" (John 15:12).

In essence, your goal is kingdom building as you advance the kingdom of God by demonstrating unconditional Godlike love towards other people. If you feel comfortable with these initial assignments, we can now determine your current status in the army. Are you an active recruit or are you a "sleepwalker?"

Are You Sleepwalking?

Did you know the word "war" appears in the King James Version of the Bible over 200 times? Have you ever wondered why God inspired men to chronicle so many wars? Did you notice that most of the wars mentioned in the New Testament are metaphoric for spiritual warfare? There is a reason for this pattern. We believe part of Jesus' message to the disciples was, "Wake Up! Stop sleepwalking through this spiritual experience. You are at war. You are under spiritual attack."

Our religious forefathers engaged in hand to hand physical battles. It is our commission to fight and win spiritual battles. Even though the disciples witnessed the marvelous works of Jesus they still found it hard to comprehend who He was or the meaning of His life (Matthew 8:23–27; 16:6–11). We can imagine Jesus was somewhat frustrated by His disciples' inability or unwillingness to believe they were at war.

At times, ministers find themselves expressing the same words from the pulpit. They have to ask their members every now and then: "Are you sleepwalking? Have you read the story? Do you know who God is and what He did for you? Do you know there is an ongoing war between the divine and the demonic?"

Let us remind you. This is spiritual warfare. The enemy wishes to sift you (Luke 22:31). First Peter 5:8 tells us, "Be sober, be vigilant; because your adversary the devil, as a roaring lion, walketh about, seeking whom he may devour." The devil is on the prowl—trying to keep your soul from eternal life.

If you really believed a lion was loose in your neighborhood, looking to devour you and your family, you would immediately be on the alert. We're sure you would warn your neighbors, devise a plan and tell everyone to be on the lookout. Isn't it equally important to protect your soul? "For what shall it profit a man, if he shall gain the whole world, and lose his own soul?" (Mark 8:36).

Now that we've established that truth, let's move on. An important starting point for the Christian disciple or the person who has joined the Army of the Lord, is to acknowledge certain realities:

- You will be attacked by the enemy (Job 1:7).
- You will be persecuted for Jesus' sake (John 15:20–21).
- You will have enemies (Luke 6:27).
- Your faith will be tested (Hebrews 11:6; James 2:17).
- Your "friends" will betray you (Matthew 24:10).

Can you handle these truths? If you are sleepwalking, you pose absolutely no threat to the enemy. In fact, the enemy might use you on occasion, especially since he has no reason to attack your life. Imagine an unarmed soldier walking across enemy lines acting like he is not a soldier. He doesn't even know his own identity. Why would he be a threat? What harm could he do?

One way to determine if you are sleepwalking is to notice your surroundings. If you are a part of a crowd that continues to invite you to partake in worldly activities, you have not set yourself apart. They do not recognize your uniform. Are you carrying your weapons?

> **If you are sleepwalking,**
> **you pose absolutely no threat to the enemy.**

As a Christian, you must develop a certain resolve about your relationship with God. Will you allow the devil to separate you from the love of Christ? "Shall tribulation, or distress, or persecution, or famine, or nakedness, or peril, or sword?" (Romans 8:35). If you are fully committed to your relationship with God, then you can say with confidence, "That neither death, nor life, nor angels, nor principalities, nor powers, nor things present, nor things to come, Nor height, nor depth, nor any other creature, shall be able to separate us [me] from the love of God, which is in Christ Jesus our Lord" (Romans 8: 38–39).

Despite the fact that you may be sleepwalking, you will be held accountable for what you know and for your actions (or inaction in this case). Therefore, we strongly advise you to wake up! It is time to "awake out of sleep" (Romans 13:11).

We encourage you to experience your walk with Christ with open eyes and a willing spirit. We welcome you to experience things no carnal mind will believe. We promise you God will do things no human being can do. Welcome to the Army of the Lord!

CHAPTER 2

SURRENDER

YOU MUST GIVE UP

*Now be ye not stiffnecked, as your fathers were,
but yield yourselves unto the LORD, and enter
into his sanctuary, which he hath sanctified for
ever: and serve the LORD your God, that the
fierceness of his wrath may turn away from you.*
—2 Chronicles 30:8

It may seem odd to begin a discussion about going into battle by first talking about surrender. However, in order to win spiritual battles, you must give your life to Christ. You must humble yourself and surrender all that you are to Christ. If you were "born in the church" then you should rededicate your life to Christ. Regardless of where you are in your church-going history, you must:

1. *Confess*: I am a sinner (Romans 3:23).

2. *Worship*: He is worthy of all the glory (Revelation 4:11).

3. ***Decrease***: God is in control of my life (John 3:30).

4. ***Believe***: I can defeat my enemies (Luke 10:19).

The songwriters put it perfectly when they wrote:

All to Jesus I surrender,
All to Him I freely give;
I will ever love and trust Him,
In His presence daily live.
All to Jesus I surrender,
Humbly at His feet I bow;
Worldly pleasures all forsaken,
Take me, Jesus, take me now.
All to Jesus I surrender,
Make me, Savior, wholly Thine;
Let me feel the Holy Spirit,
Truly know that Thou art mine.
All to Jesus I surrender,
Lord, I give myself to Thee;
Fill me with Thy love and power,
Let Thy blessings fall on me.
I surrender all.[1]

What does it mean to surrender all? It means to hand over everything. When soldiers surrender to the enemy, they hand over their weapons, tactical information and sometimes property. God may require the same from you. When the wealthy young ruler asked Jesus how he could attain eternal life, Jesus answered, "If thou wilt be perfect, go and sell that thou hast, and give to the poor, and thou shalt have treasure in heaven: and come and follow me" (Matthew 19:21). As you may recall, the wealthy young ruler declined the offer and went away sorrowful

(Matthew 19:22). He was not ready to surrender all of who he was and make Christ the center of his life.

Soldiers who surrender are in no position to negotiate. Some people try to bargain with God. You might say, "Well, I'll give up this bad habit but I'm too addicted to this other thing to give it up." You must have enough faith to believe God can deliver you from all of your weaknesses. It really is that simple. You must believe! "But without faith it is impossible to please him: for he that cometh to God must believe that he is, and that he is a rewarder of them that diligently seek him" (Hebrews 11:6). You have to want to be right! Otherwise, you will fall into the same pattern of sin that you were partaking in when you were part of the world.

Raising one's hands is a universal sign of surrender or relinquishing control to another. Spiritually, you must do the same thing—relinquish control to God by surrendering your heart, mind, and soul to Him. Now you know why some Christians raise their arms and look up when they are praising God. Picture the scene of a soldier surrendering to the more powerful army. Many Christians raise their hands in surrender to God saying:

I give up.
I cannot make it on my own.
Help me God.
Take control of my situation.
Heal my body.
Take away my addiction.
Give me the desire to live.
I give it all to you, God.
I surrender.

Admit your problems to God in prayer. If you have faith the size of a mustard seed, He will deliver you from the strongholds in your life (Mark 10:52; Luke 7:50; 8:48). Remember, God has given you a measure of faith. It is left up to you to develop your faith. Take hold of your faith, get in touch with your deepest emotions about your situation and spend some time alone with God.

If you feel sorrowful, don't fight these emotions. Crying is not a sign of weakness. Emotions capture the human condition and will draw you closer to God. When God starts knocking on the door of your heart, open it. You are now well on your way to surrendering your all to Christ.

Some Christians refer to a sorrowful time in their lives as their "midnight." Your midnight could come at any time of the day. If you have been going through a difficult time, you may have been avoiding these feelings but when you surrender your heart to God, you will feel free. The following are words of inspiration that we hope will speak to your situation and encourage you to spend some devotional time with God, surrendering all to Him.

When Your Midnight Comes at 4 A.M.

Sometimes you have to get in touch with
    that emotion.

You spend your days keeping busy, just to avoid
    that emotion
You volunteer your time helping others, just to
    avoid *that emotion*
You shop 'til you drop, just to avoid *that emotion*

You hang out with your friends, just to avoid
    that emotion
You sleep all day, just to avoid *that emotion*
You cook, clean, and comfort loved ones, just to
    avoid *that emotion*

When your work is done
When your volunteering is over
When the malls close
When your friends go home
When you wake up
When your chores are completed

When your guard is down
You look around
    And it's 4 o'clock in the morning

A tear rolls down your cheek
At first, it startles you
But then another follows
And then you realize that sooner or later
    You were bound to meet *that emotion*

It has been calling you all day
It has been calling you all week
It's been tugging at you for months

It's okay. Let your guard down.
Call Him up. Let it out.
Get in touch with *that emotion*.

"And God shall wipe away all tears from their eyes;
and there shall be no more death, neither sorrow, nor
crying, neither shall there be any more pain: for the
former things are passed away" (Revelation 21:4).

11

Time Alone

Sometimes we just need to be alone:
    alone with our thoughts
    alone with our weaknesses
    alone with our sins and our transgressions

Sometimes we just need to be alone:
    alone to cry for having evil thoughts
    alone to ponder our weaknesses
    alone to face our sins and transgressions

Sometimes we just need to be alone:
    alone to ask God to clarify our thoughts
    alone to ask God to strengthen us where we are
        weak
    alone to ask God to forgive our sins and
        transgressions

When you are confronting your negative thoughts, remember the invitation to abundant life described in Isaiah 55:7–8: "Let the wicked forsake his way, and the unrighteous man his thoughts: and let him return unto the LORD, and he will have mercy upon him; and to our God, for he will abundantly pardon. For my thoughts are not your thoughts, neither are your ways my ways, saith the LORD."

When you are recognizing your weaknesses, remember the inspiring words of Paul: "And he said unto me, My grace is sufficient for thee: for my strength is made perfect in weakness. Most gladly therefore will I rather glory in my infirmities, that the power of Christ may rest upon me" (2 Corinthians 12:9).

When you are acknowledging your sins and transgressions, remember you are not alone. "For all have sinned, and come short of the glory of God (Romans 3:23).

Although spending time alone can make you feel like an undeserving sinner, remember the Holy Spirit is always with you. "But the Comforter, which is the Holy Ghost, whom the Father will send in my name, he shall teach you all things, and bring all things to your remembrance, whatsoever I have said unto you. Peace I leave with you, my peace I give unto you: not as the world giveth, give I unto you. Let not your heart be troubled, neither let it be afraid" (John 14:26–27).

Note

1. J.W. Van DeVenter and W.S. Weeden. 1896. "I Surrender All," Hymn #354 in The United Methodist Hymnal. Nashville, TN: The United Methodist Publishing House, 1989.

CHAPTER 3

BOOT CAMP

Proclaim ye this among the Gentiles; Prepare war, wake up the mighty men, let all the men of war draw near; let them come up: Beat your plowshares into swords and your pruning hooks into spears: let the weak say, I am strong.
—Joel 3:9–10

Hoorah! I Found a Church

You have found a church home. You've joined a group of baptized believers with whom you feel comfortable. You're happy, feeling relaxed. A burden has been lifted. No more searching here and there for a church. But wait. Don't take your shoes off and don't get comfortable in those pews. The church is not your home. You are in a place that is designed to prepare you to be a soldier—a soldier in the Army of the Lord. You are in boot camp.

In the secular world, the civilian is transformed into a soldier at boot camp. The first piece of business is to shed personal identity. In fact, initiates are instructed to refer to

15

themselves in third person as recruits. Some will walk around saying, "this recruit feels ..." or "this recruit thinks ..." and so on. This practice serves to remind civilians of their low status in the group. They have no rank. They have no skills. They are in boot camp to be made into new creatures (2 Corinthians 5:17).

These verbal exercises are psychological ploys that set the foundation for learning. The leaders of the regiment (or drill instructors) are now in a position to teach since the individuals who stand before them have verbally and outwardly agreed that they are empty vessels waiting to be filled—willing to learn. Christian recruits are required to take the same pathway.

The Bible tells us to submit to leadership. If you believe the Holy Spirit has led you to join a particular church body under the leadership of the current shepherd, then act like a recruit. Recruits must learn to taper their aggressive tendencies and make themselves available for leadership roles. You must seek God's guidance during every step of your journey—including your place in the ministry. For example, just because you have a talent God used at another church (for example, choir director) does not mean God wants you to use the same talent in this new body of believers.

> Recruits must learn to taper their aggressive tendencies and make themselves available for leadership roles.

Recruits are not busybodies. Recruits are humble and they trust their leaders (James 4:10; Proverbs 16:19). You will see all kinds of interesting things and meet all kinds of interesting people within the body. Ask God to control your tongue while you're learning more about Him and your fellow recruits (James 3:8). God can give you spiritual discernment.

Once you've completed your season in boot camp, you will become a disciple and be in one accord, of one mind, with your leadership (Phillipians 1:27; 2:2; 3:16). Just have a willing mind. Submit yourself to leadership. Follow the leader. "If ye be willing and obedient, ye shall eat the good of the land: But if ye refuse and rebel, ye shall be devoured with the sword: for the mouth of the LORD hath spoken it" (Isaiah 1:19–20).

Basic Training

There will be many traps set for you in boot camp. Remember, Satan knows the Scriptures (Matthew 4:6) and he will continue to try to recruit you for his side while you are still learning the basics—hence you must stay sharp during your basic training. You must stay focused.

Traps are set while the soldier is trying to pass a series of tests. Tactical exercises are a part of basic training and usually include:

1. tests of endurance
2. problem-solving abilities
3. character-building
4. weapons of war

Tactical Exercise #1: Endurance

It is safe to say that you, the Christian recruit, will face tests similar to that of a soldier. Your endurance will be evaluated by your ability to meet the demands of being a Christian. Initially, this can involve completing the classes required by your church ministry or being a faithful disciple by giving your time, talents and treasures.

Just as a real soldier, you will get physically tired. Unlike the soldier in the world who is trying to crush his enemy, you must remember the battle is the Lord's (1 Samuel 17:47; 2 Chronicles 20:15). For this reason, fight like you have won the battle. God will renew your strength.

As in the secular army, where men and women are trained according to their skills and interests, God has provided the body of believers with talents. Do not hide your talent. Let it be used for the edification of others (Matthew 25:15–28). Your personal abilities can be used to advance the kingdom of heaven. There may be times when you are not certain about your talents. Ask God to reveal His plan for your life (Jeremiah 29:11) and He will direct your paths. In the meantime, be faithful and support those around you by showing up to church services on time and engaging in volunteer work that helps the less fortunate.

The treasures you are expected to contribute to the church are tithes and offerings. Tithing is a simple matter for some and a challenge for others. Again, the Bible is very clear on the way in which the church is to be supported (Malachi 3:10) and our role in fulfilling God's mission for the church. Some people fall short of tithing and are tripped up by decoys. On the battlefield, the enemy will use a decoy to distract the opponent. There is no victory (or blessing) in decoys. If you are giving monetarily through fund raisers instead of paying your tithes and offerings, you have fallen for a decoy.

As you grow in Christ you will come to understand that the sacrifices you make are your reasonable service to the ministry (Romans 12:1). Armies need resources to make the men and women in uniform successful soldiers.

The sacrifices you make through faithful stewardship will be rewarded by God.

Tactical Exercise #2: Problem-Solving

Your problem-solving abilities will be challenged as you face issues particular to the body of believers you have joined forces with or by the tests Satan has devised for you. At this point, it is important that you feel comfortable talking with your church leaders (bishops, ministers, deacons, elders). Spiritual leaders are often experienced enough to separate the issues and direct you in the way you should go.

Be certain that your leaders provide biblical references for the solutions to your problems. Your goal here is to become an independent soldier rather than a dependent recruit. You should be able to mark your growth in Christ by your ability to solve certain problems.

We encounter several kinds of problems that are similar to those described in the natural world under the discipline of mathematics: (1) area (2) work and (3) motion. Don't get discouraged. Remember, God will meet you at the point of your human need.

Area Problems

Some people have difficulties in certain areas of life: finances, health, relationships. These issues can be very difficult to resolve, they may affect other areas of one's life and often require a great deal of emotional adjustment.

Financial problems are common among many people. Low wages accompanied by increasing inflation, sudden unemployment and unexpected life circumstances are situations that can lead to financial stress. Health concerns can be a distraction from kingdom-building. Of course, different types of health problems surface at certain stages of life but most of them can be burdensome. Many of the problems we face in relationships are linked to finances and health. For example, arguments about money are the most common reason given by couples seeking divorce. Even high-income couples have frequent disagreements about managing the household finances. The Holy Bible provides a solution to these particular area problems: "Ask, and it shall be given you; seek, and ye shall find; knock, and it shall be opened unto you" (Matthew 7:7).

In addition to our faith, God has provided opportunities to learn more about managing our finances, and increasing medical knowledge has given us a greater sense of control over a variety of health outcomes. In fact, God expects us to be good stewards over all of His blessings, including our income, wealth and health.

Besides physical health problems, you may also be distracted by mental health concerns. Twenty percent of Americans suffer from mood disorders such as depression and anxiety. Feelings of despair and loneliness are signs of depression. While a number of the area problems we mentioned can make you feel depressed and alone, your reaction is key. The enemy will try to convince you that you are worthless. Satan wants to make you feel like you are alone, you have no friends and no one understands the real you. This is where the scripture regarding the foe is so important. Remember, you wrestle not against flesh and blood, but against principalities, powers, rulers of darkness and spiritual wickedness (Ephesians 6:12). In other words, the devil will mess with your mind.

Imagine a puzzle, if you will, with a missing piece. You try to fit all kinds of pieces into it; you continue to search for the missing piece. Tony (Tonya) looks like he'll fit, but when you try, he turns out to be the wrong shape. Brian (Brooke) doesn't work out and neither does Kevin (Katie). You just knew Kevin (Katie) would fill that void, but you still feel lonely. In fact, you may be married and still feel lonely. Guess what? *Jesus has the power to complete who you are.*

I'm not pretty enough
Jesus has the power to complete who you are

I'm not wealthy enough
Jesus has the power to complete who you are

I'm not thin enough
Jesus has the power to complete who you are

I'm not smart enough
Jesus has the power to complete who you are

I'm not spiritual enough
Jesus has the power to complete who you are

Jesus fills the gap, no matter how big—no matter what the shape of your missing piece. The divine power of the Holy Spirit is the only power that has the inspired ability to fill the gaps in your life, to complete who you are. Hallelujah!

> **Jesus has the power to complete who you are.**

A common response to feelings of loneliness is to seek friends among the Christian church family. Although you should surround yourself with those who have a strong faith in God, you must not rely on your own abilities to determine who should be a part of your life. Again, ask God to put positive people in your life. If you are not cautious, you may meet a lot of church-going folk who allow demonic, rather than divine, spirits to rule their lives. People can never take the place of God. If you make people the source of your joy, your spiritual side will wither.

Work Problems

Area problems can become work problems—which means that they will require some work in order to be resolved. The key to solving work problems is the amount of time it takes to complete a task. Some problems can be so personal that we hesitate to share them with others and carry the burden alone. One consequence of this decision is that it takes us longer than necessary to work through these problems. The Bible provides a solution to work problems: find a comrade—a prayer partner. "For where two or three are gathered together in my name, there am I in the midst of them" (Matthew 18:20, also see Galatians 6:2).

In the secular army, many weapons cannot be completely loaded and fired without some assistance. In a war-like situation, we often need someone else to knock the target out so that we, the ground forces, can advance. When Christians combine forces against the enemy, we form a two-prong attack—like Paul and Silas (Acts 16:25).

Motion Problems

There are other types of problems you will face in your walk with God. You may be moving too slow or you may be rushing things in your spiritual walk with Christ. Ask yourself, how much distance am I covering over what period of time? Perhaps you should re-examine the rate of growth in your spiritual life. What is the solution to these problems? God wills "That ye be not slothful, but followers of them who through faith and patience inherit the promises" (Hebrews 6:12).

If you are not active in any ministry in your church, you are being slothful. You need to graduate from the "pew ministry." God has called you to be an active recruit. He does not expect you to take a leave of absence as soon as you sign up for duty! Find out where you may be needed in the church. Perhaps volunteers are needed to serve food to the homeless on weekends. Maybe a disabled member of the church needs a ride once a month to church services.

Take time out to hear from God about the pace at which you are progressing as a Christian. Once you become active, try not to respond like the Pharisees and Sadducees by announcing your good deeds to others. "Let another man praise thee, and not thine own mouth; a stranger, and not thine own lips" (Proverbs 27:2). Jesus was a humble servant. Pattern your walk after Him.

It is also possible to move too fast in the body of Christ. The reason some people want to move quickly is because the good news of our resurrected Savior is very exciting. The name of Jesus has always generated excitement. The Gospels are full of examples.

The problem with moving too fast, however, is the potential to neglect other parts of life such as jobs, families or school work. God expects you to be a well-rounded Christian. Avoid becoming so spiritually minded that you are of no earthly good! Christian recruits who move too fast have usually ignored part of their basic training.

Those who move too fast also run the risk of burn-out. They join too many ministries without having consulted God for His guidance or they evangelize and minister to others without having a strong spiritual foundation.

Perhaps you are active in your church ministry but are not being recognized for your good deeds. If you have become disillusioned with your walk in Christ don't become an MIA—missing in action. After reading *Preparing for Battle* you should be able to pinpoint what part of the basics you have not mastered. Go back to training camp before the enemy's attack overwhelms you. Don't give up—your blessing is on the way!

Other Types of Motion Problems

Dreams. Sigmund Freud, an atheist, believed that every dream had some underlying message. Needless to say, if Freud were alive today he would not offer a spiritual interpretation of dreams. In general, dreams capture unresolved anxieties—issues we have neglected to address while we were awake. At other times, important information can be embedded in dreams (Jeremiah 29:8).

As a Christian recruit, you must understand that the spiritual realm includes divine and demonic forces. Both will operate in your subconscious and manifest themselves in dreams. How are you to know the difference? *The Bible*. In the Scriptures, dreams are always followed by an interpretation. If the message in your dream is not scripturally sound or does not promote the kingdom of God as commissioned in the Holy Word, then your dream should not be spiritually interpreted. Perhaps you should keep a journal, write down your dreams, and see how God moves in your life as you grow closer to Him. It can become a testimony for the awesomeness of God.

The Calling. A common phrase used among some Christians is "I have a calling on my life" or someone will say, "a prophet told me there is a calling on my life." All those within the body of Christ have a calling on their lives. Jesus said, "Ye have not chosen me, but I have chosen you, and ordained you, that ye should go and bring forth fruit, and that your fruit should remain" (John 15:16). In other words, we have all been commissioned to go out and spread the gospel of Jesus Christ (2 Timothy 1:9; 1 Corinthians 1:26–27).

Many people desire the spotlight of being in the highest position of the church (minister, preacher, bishop, pastor) rather than being a servant in the house of the Lord. Everyone has an assignment within the church. The church body, like a human body, consists of many parts. Ask God to reveal the part you are to play in your faith community and always let your calling and election be sure (2 Peter 1:10). "And he gave some, apostles; and some, prophets; and some, evangelists; and some, pastors and teachers; For the perfecting of the saints, for the work of the ministry, for the edifying of the body of Christ" (Ephesians 4:11–12).

> Everyone has an assignment within the church.

To summarize, Christians face a variety of problems (area, work and motion). Some of these problems may turn into burdens if they are not immediately addressed. The following is a general strategy used by mathematicians to solve problems. It is well suited for Christians in dealing with the problems of everyday life.

1. Become familiar with the problem situation.

2. Translate the problem situation to spiritual language or symbolism.

3. Use your spiritual knowledge to find a possible solution.

4. Check to see if your possible solution actually fits the problem situation and is a true solution to the problem.

As a child of God, you can expect more problems in the future. Christians are subject to all the problems faced by mankind. Having a relationship with God does not guarantee a care-free life. Take great comfort in knowing, however, that God is always with you. He is a problem solver.

A word of caution—your problems may seem more complicated as you grow spiritually. There will be times when Satan will try to convince you that your problems cannot be solved. Just remember what Jesus said: "Come unto me, all ye that labour and are heavy laden, and I will give you rest. Take my yoke upon you, and learn of me; for I am meek and lowly in heart: and ye shall find rest unto your souls. For my yoke is easy, and my burden is light" (Matthew 11:28–30).

Whenever you are faced with a problem, you should pray and wait for God to speak to you (Hebrews 4:15–16). At times, He will drop the answer into your spirit (or in layman's terms, it will come to you). Sometimes He will direct you to a scripture. At other times He will send a Christian your way who will speak to your situation. Their words of encouragement should be consistent with the Scriptures and should speak to your spiritual side (it should feel right). Talk to God about your problems and He will put them in perspective. When you remember that

God reigns supreme, everything else will become background noise.

> When you remember that God reigns supreme, everything else will become background noise.

Walking with God can be a challenge. You must be ready to talk about the stormy times in your life for the purpose of helping someone else. This puts you in a position to help another recruit who may face the same storm. You must turn your private storm into a public service announcement.

The Private Storm

To everything there is a season, and a time to every purpose under the heaven (Ecclesiastes 3:1).

Hugo. Nino. Bonnie. Most of us are familiar with one of these storms. We heard about the gusting winds, high tides and damage they caused to the shorelines, trees and personal property. Storms usually leave a trail behind them. We know when an area has been hit by a storm.

But what about a *private storm*? Or is that an oxymoron? Can someone really have a *private storm*? Most of us think we can. That's why we refuse to cry in church. We'd rather wait until we get to our vehicles or we're behind the closed doors of our bedrooms. We hesitate to say "amen" when the minister speaks directly to our circumstances or we refuse to raise our hands when someone stands at the podium and asks if they can get a witness.

There are some storms that blow us away. Strong winds can blow, knock us off our feet and leave us in a daze. We dare not share this story of the *phantom wind*. We've decided not to reveal that private storm.

Water usually follows or occurs during a storm. We hear torrential rainfalls during a storm. Like the gushing of water from a faucet, our eyes often betray the fact that we are going through a private storm. The tears flow when we are home alone or droplets may fall, unexpectedly, in the middle of a conversation. They may all come down at once when someone says the "wrong thing" but we can't do too much gushing, for then we may reveal we are going through a storm, a private storm.

And don't start leaning. That's really when someone might notice we're going through a hard time. Trees lean in a storm; some of them bounce back, others fall. We dare not lean; stand up tall, lest someone finds out we're going through a private storm.

We're here to tell you that no storm is really private. A storm leaves a trail. It marks its territory. It tells onlookers that a storm passed this way. The teary eyes or leaning posture will give you away every time.

You may think you're going through a private storm, but really you aren't. Storms affect those around you, your family members and friends. Storms are a part of a larger weather pattern. They tend to be seasonal in nature and they hit certain areas (of your life) more than others.

Another characteristic of many storms is that they can be unpredictable. You don't always know when they will hit. Once they arrive, you don't know how long they will last. Once you are in a storm, you never know how far ahead of you the storm is and in what direction it is traveling. All you know is that you're in a storm! You may wonder, should I continue forward or turn back? Sometimes, the answer is neither. Just keep still. "Wait on the LORD: be of good courage" (Psalms 27:14). God will still your storm. Remember how He spoke peace to the storm in Luke 8:22–24?

This unpredictability is why a private storm should be publicized. You should tell somebody—maybe not everybody—but somebody. Inform the public. If a tornado touched down in your neighborhood you would feel compelled to call the media. Perhaps you could adopt the format of a public service announcement:

Warning, warning.

Storm ahead!

Heavy rainfall.

Storm clouds may rise.

Strong winds may blow.

Take cover and be prepared.

Whenever you find yourself in the storm, do not panic. God is in control. Remember, *He's your shelter in the time of storms.* He will quiet your fears, mend your broken heart, bless your finances and heal your body.

Having been through a storm you can tell somebody else about it. You can describe to them what it looked like when it was approaching and what it felt like while you were in the midst of it. You can tell how you felt after it was over and what preparations you've made for the next storm. You can give an account of how often you prayed, what conversations you avoided and what scriptures you found most useful. Amen?

Tactical Exercise #3: Character-Building

As a new recruit, you will meet others in the body of Christ who challenge your character. They will stir up emotions you never knew you had—some will provoke you. This is another opportunity for growth. God's strength is made perfect in our weakness (2 Corinthians 12:9).

There are other traps that you should be aware of that can challenge your character. One trap is actual conversation. You might decide to seek the advice of a fellow Christian soldier or express your joy about some particular event in your life. The trap to avoid is the extended conversation. Don't become a gossip monger. It is easy to begin a conversation with a question and find yourself talking about others. This is a sure sign the conversation you are having is not pleasing to God. Cut it off—quickly. Use your speech to encourage others and yourself. Your conversation will reflect your character.

As a Christian recruit, you must accept the fact that not everyone in the church is interested in kingdom-building. This is sad, but true. Just as civilians join the military for a variety of reasons, individuals join churches for their own reasons. Some people join because their friends joined. Some join because they're searching for a new adventure. And then, be warned, there are spies in the camp—people whose sole purpose is to find out what is going on and report back to others.

Regardless of the motives of other recruits, the good news is that once people are in the body, they can be recruited for the right purposes. Every church body has saints and ain'ts. Saints are individuals seeking a closer relationship with God. Ain'ts are those who are looking for the blessings of Jesus. Ain'ts only seek the blessings of God while saints seek the One who blesses. Pray for the strength of the saints and the conversion of the ain't's.

> Pray for the strength of the saints and the conversion of the ain'ts.

Love will bind you together with your church family. Remember, Jesus showed compassion for the multitudes who followed Him, even those who simply wanted the fish and loaves. You must demonstrate a similar love for your fellow recruits. Open your heart to others but protect your mind and soul from demonic spirits by using your weaponry.

Tactical Exercise #4: Weapons of War

In order to win spiritual battles, you must learn how to use your weapons. Although man acts within the flesh to access these weapons, the fact is, "We do not war after the flesh: (For the weapons of our warfare are not carnal, but mighty through God to the pulling down of strong holds;) Casting down imaginations, and every high thing that exalteth itself against the knowledge of God, and bringing into captivity every thought to the obedience of Christ" (2 Corinthians 10:3–5).

For the Christian, the two most important weapons of war are prayer and the Bible. Fervent prayer and the written Word of God are sufficient weapons against the enemy, but you must learn how to use these weapons effectively.

Prayer. The Christian must pray. Prayer is not an option—it is a command. "Men ought always to pray, and not to faint" (Luke 18:1). Prayer is an appeal to God. It is a two-way communication street between mankind and

God. Once you recognize that God wants to hear from you on a consistent basis, you will be on your way to becoming a healthy Christian soldier—an effective witness for Christ.

Prayer is multidimensional. It includes worship, confession and thanksgiving. Prayer also serves multiple functions. Christians are expected to pray for others and intercede on their behalf. "But I say unto you, Love your enemies, bless them that curse you, do good to them that hate you, and pray for them which despitefully use you, and persecute you" (Matthew 5:44).

The Moms-In-Touch Ministry at Sherwood Oaks Christian Church provides an excellent example of one way to put prayer to work. Once a week, for one hour, the mothers of school-aged children gather around the kitchen table at a member's house and pray out loud for the children, teachers and administrators in schools. Each mother has agreed to pray for five schools, so within a month, twenty schools and hundreds of children, teachers and administrators have been brought to God's attention. Within a year, 240 schools and thousands of children, teachers and administrators have been brought to God's attention. What do you think will happen? Remember, God answers prayer.

Once you make prayer a part of your daily routine, you will find yourself talking to God throughout the day—regardless of the situations you might face. You are now in a position to use prayer as a weapon against the enemy. When the doctor gives you a negative report, you will feel comfortable telling him or her that your God is a great physician whom you will consult on the matter.

An interesting study was described in a recent news story. Scientists are trying to understand why patients who pray have better health outcomes and faster recovery times than patients who do not pray. Some things cannot be explained in the natural world. Christians understand "prayer puts God to work."[1]

To gain a deeper understanding of prayer and the power of prayer, attend prayer conferences or spiritual retreats that are sponsored by your church or churches in your area. Most people do not hesitate to register for conferences that focus on professional growth. As a Christian, be equally attentive to your spiritual growth. You must feed your spiritual side or it will starve. Remember, a delay in your prayer request is not necessarily a denial. God answers prayers. Just ask King Hezekiah (2 Kings 20:5–6).

Bible Study. The Word of God is the most powerful weapon against the enemy. "For the word of God is quick, and powerful, and sharper than any twoedged sword, piercing even to the dividing asunder of soul and spirit, and of the joints and marrow, and is a discerner of the thoughts and intents of the heart" (Hebrews 4:12). God commands us to hide the Word in our hearts so that we can be equipped to fight the enemy. The battles we face may include attacks against ourselves or our loved ones.

Use the Word of God to encourage yourself to continue living a Christian lifestyle and encourage those whom God puts in your life. Kingdom-building requires workers and part of the job of a soldier is to recruit others to the Army of Christ.

Attending weekly Bible study and Sunday School classes can help build your spiritual stockpile in times of distress. In your private Bible study, include additional reference guides to facilitate further explanation of the Holy Scriptures. The Holy Bible holds a number of secrets (Proverbs 25:2). In many Bible stories you will often:

1. see yourself (a part of your personality)
2. see your situation (as described in parables)
3. find a solution to your problem (through other biblical characters)
4. learn more about God (His feelings, His inclinations, His habits)

Read your Bible.

Those recruits interested in being good soldiers will learn all they can to be the best that they can be in Christ Jesus. Remember, God can be found in every volume of the Book. When food tastes good, we can't wait for the next opportunity to taste it. So it is with the Word of God—when it's good, you don't mind taking time out of your day to get some more. Don't lose your foothold on the battleground because of an empty heart or an empty belly. Read your Bible.

Our Secret Weapon: Praise & Worship

There is one weapon that you must not hesitate to use when you find yourself battling demons. During the course of a war, the opposing sides usually have at their disposal some secret weapon. For Christians, this weapon is praise & worship (Psalm 138:1–2).

You will find yourself in situations that just don't seem to make any sense. You will wonder how and when your life took this peculiar turn. At what point did Satan decide to put you at the top of his most wanted list? When did you become target practice? Well, if you are at this point, it's time to pull out your secret weapon—praise and worship. It may sound simple, but it works.

The reason praise and worship is a secret weapon is because Satan does not expect you to have the capacity to praise and worship God when your world is falling apart. From his viewpoint you should be cursing God. This is the best time to launch a surprise attack. When praises go up to heaven, blessings come down from heaven. Think of praise and worship as a form of guerrilla warfare.

> Think of praise and worship as a form of guerrilla warfare.

Praise. "From the rising of the sun unto the going down of the same the LORD's name is to be praised" (Psalm 113:3). It is time to put on your warrior's face. Scream. Shout! Raise your arms. Stomp your feet. Do whatever it takes to make your enemy flee! You must be willing to step outside of your comfort zone for God.

This is the time to forget all protocol. There is no time for long, lengthy prayers. You are being beaten down. You are tired. You are crying constantly. You can't seem to get a hold of this crisis. We're telling you the secret: Praise God and soon you will come out of your storm. The Israelites always sent the "praise and worship team" out on the front lines before the soldiers. The praise team set the tone for the battle. What is your battle cry?

Praising God in public is difficult for some people. This is why it is considered a form of guerrilla warfare. Most regiments revert to guerrilla tactics when they feel they are at a disadvantage against their enemies. They must devise a plan to turn their weaknesses into strengths. If you find it difficult to express yourself openly in public (in your church sanctuary, for example), ask God to help you put His word to work in your life.

The Christian who is battling demonic forces must use every weapon available in the arsenal and that includes praise and worship. Praise God for what He has done for you in the past. Praise God for what He is doing right now. Praise God for what you know He is capable of doing in the future. Just praise God! Give Him a "yet praise." I have yet to get out of this situation but I'm going to praise God anyway. We dare you to try this strategy. Sit back and watch what happens. God will intercede on your behalf. And then, worship Him.

Worship. Worship is sacred, quiet time before God. You are humbled before His presence. You have come to a place in your mind where you realize that He is God, the omnipotent, omnipresent One.

Some of us can't worship God in spirit because we are victims of carnal logic. We have been taught to rationalize every behavior. In so doing, we will reject the very idea that it is necessary to bow the head, bend the knees or lay prostrate in order to worship God. In the same manner, people will raise their arms at a sporting event and hail their favorite players (some actually worship athletes), and some people will bow down to royalty when visiting other countries.

When you think about the goodness of Jesus and the awesome power of God the Creator, your soul should cry out, "Hallelujah!" and your physical body should yield in worship.

Once you've been invited into the presence of God, you will feel comfortable worshiping God in private or public settings. Many Christians do not hesitate to bow down or lay prostrate three to five times a day! "O come, let us worship and bow down: let us kneel before the

LORD our maker" (Psalm 95:6). Let us try to express to you why we should worship Him.

Why We Should Worship Him

Let's start from a given—a premise—there is no question here—there is no question about it! We should worship Him. If you are a worshiper and you see yourself in these areas, you should loudly proclaim, "Amen, hallelujah," or "Glory be to God!"

Why We Should Worship Him. It's not a question. There's no question about it. We worship Him because:

- He accepts us just as we are.
- He loves us despite the fact that we went there ... said that ... did that.
- He heard us even though we didn't have time to listen to someone else's problems.
- He takes us from where we are to where we should be in Him.
- He sees all and knows all.
- He speaks to our circumstances, our trivial, trifling lives.
- He is mighty in battle.
- He opens doors that we didn't even realize existed.
- He's the only living God.

Why We Should Worship Him. It's not a question. There's no question about it. We worship Him because:

- With His eyes, He sees our affliction.

- With His lips, He comforts us through His word.

- With His ears, He hears our cries, especially in our midnight hour.

- With His beating heart, He feels our pain.

Why We Should Worship Him. It's not a question. There's no question about it. We worship Him because:

- He left us a gift
  A *pen-pal*, for those who like to write their thoughts to God on paper. He'll read it and relay the message.
  A *confidante*, for those who like to talk things out. You know He won't tell.
  A *comforter*, for those who get lonely and depressed. He'll tell you it's going to be alright; joy's going to come in the morning.
  A *buddy*, for those who travel to and fro, with the assurance that He's with us everywhere.
  A *healer*, for those times when the body shuts down and we invite the Spirit of the living God to touch our flesh.

And last but not least, we worship Him because:

- He is awesome
  Awesome in His creation
  Awesome in His splendor

Why We Should Worship Him. It's not a question. There's no question about it. He is the creator, after all, and we are merely the creation.

As you grow in your spiritual walk with Christ, you will learn to use prayer, the Word of God and praise and worship at the right times. These rituals activate your primary power source—the Holy Spirit. Now God will move on your behalf in the spirit realm (Matthew 16:19). Strongholds can now be torn down and God will make right some of those wrong situations in your life. Hallelujah! Praises be to God! Now you're ready to go to battle for the Lord.

Note

1. E.M. Bounds. 1996. *The Weapon of Prayer* (Whitaker House, New Kensington, PA).

CHAPTER 4

GOING OFF TO BATTLE

And he said, Hearken ye, all Judah, and ye inhabitants of Jerusalem, and thou King Jehoshaphat, Thus saith the LORD unto you, Be not afraid nor dismayed by reason of this great multitude; for the battle is not yours, but God's.

—2 Chronicles 20:15

We sing hymn after hymn suggesting that we know we are fighting a battle. A popular song within the Christian faith is "I Am On the Battlefield for My Lord." Preachers speak endlessly, and hundreds of books are written on the topic of spiritual warfare. Despite all these warnings, we wake up every morning, day after day, go through our routinized lives and get shot, maimed and often mutilated by the devil. We come home defeated, desperate and depressed. We're angry, anxious and apathetic. We just don't care anymore. Our children, who accompany us, often look messed up, too. Why? How can this happen? For the simple reason that we're in denial about the war. We refuse to accept the fact that we go off to war every day.

Now you might ask, why would somebody join the Army of the Lord if they never expected to fight? Think about it in the natural realm. While many people join the military in order to protect their country, others join for the material benefits that are offered to them. Some join for the G.I. bill and others might join to qualify for a cheaper loan on a house. Some join so that they can lose weight in boot camp. Some want to learn how to handle firearms. So it is with the body of Christ. Many people join the Army of Christ to reap the benefits of being in the "services" of the Lord. They are seeking God's hands and not His face.

When you realize that the attacks on your life are not directed towards you but Christ in you, then you will be more likely to put on your helmet (of salvation). You should wear your helmet when you go off to war. You must protect your *mind*.

> You must protect your mind.

Mine/Mind Fields

By the time a regiment, or group of soldiers, is in position to go to battle, a drill instructor has told them about the minefield. The instructor has described the field itself (usually an open area) and the different types of mines that may be planted in the field. You can imagine the instructor saying: "Well recruits, you have completed your basic training. You understand your mission. You know who the enemy is and you know how to use your weapons. It is now time for you to actually cross a battlefield. Let me describe the dangers you will face in a minefield."

In the case of the Christian recruit, it is more appropriate that we discuss the "mind" field. It is important for you to understand that the journey across this field is a faith walk (2 Corinthians 5:7). Don't forget your shield of faith.

The battles you will face will begin in your mind. The human mind remains a mystery to many scientists. The mind embodies thought processes and aspects of reasoning. Scientists have determined that certain regions of the human brain are responsible for logical thinking and emotions. These are the areas the devil has planned for strategic attacks. Let us begin with logic.

Logic

Many of us are rationalizing creatures. We seek to find a reasonable and acceptable explanation for most things found in nature. Once these explanations are found, our minds are put at ease. If we can understand something, we tend to feel like we have some control over it.

While this type of reasoning is useful in some areas of life, logical thinking can invade your walk with Christ. All along the way, as you learn, you will seek a deeper understanding. You will grapple with explanations offered by your teachers (ministers and preachers). You will have the urge to engage in debate about the origins of the universe, the crossing of the Red Sea, the birth of Christ or John's revelation on the isle of Patmos. Your mind is at work.

God wants us to be intelligent and inquisitive soldiers; Jesus was a teacher, and Peter and Paul insist that we be able to defend our belief in the Gospel (Acts 22:1; 1 Corinthians 9:3; 2 Timothy 4:16; 1 Peter 3:15). We must always be prepared to give reasons for our faith. During this period of our lives as Christians, we will rely heavily upon our ability to reason. However, when you're walking with Christ across the battlefield, you will neither see nor understand everything that happens in the field. This is a faith walk.

God left us with scriptures that should guide our questions. "But foolish and unlearned questions avoid, knowing that they do gender strifes. And the servant of the Lord must not strive; but be gentle unto all men, apt to teach, patient, In meekness instructing those that oppose themselves; if God peradventure will give them repentance to the acknowledging of the truth; And that they may recover themselves out of the snare of the devil, who are taken captive by him at his will" (2 Timothy 2:23–26). This passage of scripture reminds us that Satan can use reason and logical thinking to stunt our spiritual growth. We can actually stop growing in Christ by thinking too much! Remember, this is a faith walk.

To have any chance of winning spiritual battles, you must know when to set aside your logical thinking. "Trust in the LORD with all thine heart; and lean not unto thine own understanding" (Proverbs 3:5). You must learn when it is time to rely on spiritual guidance across the battlefield. As suggested by the Scriptures, one way for the Christian to think about this issue is in terms of what is true and what is the truth.

It May Be True, but Is It the Truth?

In our technologically-advanced society, we place a great deal of weight on scientific proof. We only believe information that can be conceptualized and confirmed. It has to be reliable and reproducible. It must be validated and verified.

This should come as no surprise. We live in an age when science has uprooted philosophy. Students approach religion as doctrine or a body of theoretical principles. Religion becomes something you have, not something you feel.

We are here to tell you that just because it's true, doesn't mean it's the truth. Let's consider the following example. How would you respond to the statement, "Fire burns." True or False?

While it may be true that what man has defined as the physical manifestation of fire is evident in the light and heat that occurs during this active phase of combustion, the truth is that there have been firelike displays that were not consistent with man's definition of fire. Just ask Brother Moses. According to Exodus 3:2, "The angel of the LORD appeared unto him in a flame of fire out of the midst of a bush: and he looked, and, behold, the bush burned with fire, and the bush was not consumed." So we have here a burning fire that does not burn nor consume a bush.

Perhaps you think one man's account isn't enough. There were no eyewitnesses to Moses' burning bush. You may be more convinced by the testimony of Brother Daniel's companions. Remember how King Nebuchadnezzar commanded his servants to heat the furnace seven times hotter than usual in order to punish three boys because they did not agree to worship the golden image of a god? We know the furnace was working because the men that took these three Hebrew boys to the furnace were killed by the fire (Daniel 3:22).

This story of deliverance from the fiery furnace also falls in direct contradiction to what we profess to know about fire. Although Shadrach, Meshach and Abednego were cast into the fiery furnace (Daniel 3:23), there was no physical evidence that they had been burned by the fire. The Bible says, "And the princes, governors, and captains, and the king's counselors, being gathered together, saw these men, upon whose bodies the fire had no power, nor was a hair on their head singed, neither were their coats changed, nor the smell of fire had passed on them" (Daniel 3:27). In other words, while it is true that fire burns, the truth is fire does not have to burn.

When we place the words "true" or "false" as diametrically opposite forces, we put ourselves in a position to rely on scientific evidence. We enter a cognitive realm where there is no gray area. It is either true or it is false. But the truth does not operate on this playing field. The truth rises above this simple dichotomy. The truth cannot be found in mathematical formulas or dictionaries. The only information you will find in these sources is what man has determined is true.

If you're searching for the truth, you have to read God's Holy Word (John 17:17). When you rely on the truth, you can be delivered from a fiery furnace. In your search for the truth, you come to understand how Jesus served as an intermediary between God and man. Jesus said, "I am the way, the truth, and the life: no man cometh unto the Father, but by me" (John 14:6).

Reason can be treason in the spirit realm. A soldier convicted of treason has defected to the other side. He has decided to serve the enemy. There is no one more despised by a regiment than a defector. Those convicted of treason are often remembered in our annals of history.

Logical thinking can be used as a trick by the enemy. This is a crafty trick. Even as you're reading these lines, your mind is questioning this proposition. "Beware lest any man spoil you through philosophy and vain deceit, after the tradition of men, after the rudiments of the world, and not after Christ" (Colossians 2:8).

> Logical thinking can be used as a trick by the enemy.

Not everyone will recognize the difference between what is true and what is the truth. As a Christian soldier, you must learn the difference. So:

- If your doctors tell you that you have an incurable disease, tell them, "That may be true, but it's not necessarily the truth." (Matthew 8:2–3; 9:2, 20–22).

- If your employer tells you that you do not have the skills to move up in the company, tell him or her, "That may be true, but it's not necessarily the truth." (Matthew 7:7).

- If the bank tells you that you don't have the right credentials or enough assets to purchase material goods (for example, a car or home), tell them, "That may be true, but it's not necessarily the truth." (1 Samuel 16:12–13)

Don't get caught up in what is true or false. Believe in God's word. Believe the truth.

Emotions

Another dimension of your mind that you will wrestle with (at least until you get to the point where you're willing to admit this is a problem) in this Christian walk is emotion. This can be a touchy subject with some Christians. Some denominations encourage full emotional expression of the goodness of Jesus. Others say, "It doesn't take all that." It is not our goal to tell you the level of emotion you should feel or how you should express yourself in church services. We want to warn you of some of the traps Satan has set for this part of your mind.

Let us begin by saying that Jesus showed emotion. When He found people selling goods in the temple, He became angry (Matthew 21:12). When He heard His friend was dead, He was sad (John 11:35). When the disciples didn't understand the parables, He became frustrated (Matthew 15:16). When the multitudes needed healing, He had compassion (Matthew 15:32). When He realized the goodness of God was available to the young and old, He was glad (Luke 10:21).

Jesus told the multitudes to rejoice and be glad about the kingdom of God. His disciples rejoiced (Luke 19:37). What image comes to your mind when you see a group of people rejoicing? God didn't give us emotions to bury them.

Emotions are a part of the human condition. They can be used to glorify God or to glorify Satan. As a Christian, you must become sensitive enough to the move of the Holy Spirit that you do not find yourself expressing emotions simply because others around you are emotional or suppressing your emotions because others around you are unemotional. You should be led by the Spirit to either glorify God with a loud voice or worship Him through silent expression. If you are not being led by the Spirit, your sacrifice of praise will not be received by God. You are wasting your time. You have become a robot, not a soldier. Beware!

People who have been overexposed to logical reasoning enter into a sanctuary carrying that baggage. Some refuse to raise their hands as the minister ushers in the Holy Spirit. Others refuse to say amen because they've learned that such behavior is part of a call-and-response pattern that members of the lower social classes follow out of tradition. If this sounds like you, you're missing the point. Satan is playing with your mind.

God is the head of this army. In order to work through you, He must have a personal relationship with you. Of course, God knows you. The problem is you don't really know Him and you're not familiar with His voice. In order to open a two-way conversation, you will need to take off your mask and be real with God.

When you have a close friend, you feel and express the range of human emotions with that person. God does not expect you to communicate with Him cerebrally or telepathically. God expects you to open your mouth and proclaim with a loud voice that Jesus is the risen Savior. That fact alone will make some people scream, shout, run, dance, do flips or swing from the chandeliers.

Can you imagine what people would do if they found out Jesus loves them unconditionally? Can you imagine what people would do if you told them He's a healer? Emotional expression can usher in or hinder your blessing. Let the Holy Spirit move you!

If you cannot move past the thought of crossing the field (putting your logic and emotions in perspective), you will not survive the different types of mines that are buried in the field. Remember, victory is on the other side of the mind field. Now, are you ready to go across?

The March

Most of us are familiar with the basic chant soldiers learn in the military—left, left, left, right, left. As the soldier progresses through basic training, the chants become more complicated. Chants signify solidarity or unity within a regiment. Everyone is in one accord, marching to the same beat. Every church has its own rhythm. All soldiers within the church should learn to march to the beat of the drummer (your leader).

At times, God may use you to introduce a new beat to your congregation. Even in these instances, God expects you to be orderly when you make suggestions to your church leaders. If the Holy Spirit leads you in this direction, there will be little resistance.

There is something else about the march you need to know. There is an emotional component to the march. Because the march is often put to the sound of music, some people will lose sight of their mission and get carried away with the march. This is another way the enemy tries to trick the soldier. Perhaps you've noticed that some of your church members are very emotional. They are emotionally charged during praise and worship or when the choir is singing. They get excited when the music is playing. When that particular part of the program is over, they look bored and disinterested in the next stage—weaponry training. Suddenly there is no enthusiasm about the preaching of the Word that is about to come forth and no consideration for intercessory prayer. The fun part of being in the army is over since the march has ended.

Soldiers who only get excited when the music is playing are usually those who have failed basic training. They have not come to a full understanding of their

> Soldiers who only get excited when
> the music is playing
> are usually those who have failed basic training.

mission. They underestimate the power of the enemy and they do not know how or when to use their weapons. These are the same soldiers who will have a good time screaming and shouting on Sunday morning but be depressed by Monday night. If you recognize this pattern among someone in your regiment, pull them aside and invite them to attend Bible study or become a part of your prayer circle. You never want to see a comrade fall into the hands of the enemy. Help them to be all they can be, in Christ Jesus!

It Is the Spirit of... and You Must Conquer It!

When our self-esteem is attacked, we respond in somewhat predictable ways. The ways we respond when we're feeling like we are no good at all can be captured in terms of the "spirits" to which we yield. These are the traps of the enemy—the type of mines he has planted in the field.

When soldiers are informed that an area they will be covering may have been set with mines, they will slow their pace and move very carefully and deliberately through the field. They do not run. They do not engage in mindless chatter—or idle conversation. The unit is typically extremely quiet so they can detect the presence of a mine. Soldiers know if they make one wrong move, a mine can blow; therefore, soldiers survey the field and prepare themselves for this form of warfare.

When you wake up in the morning, you should give honor and praise to God. You should acknowledge that you are still a part of the Army of the Lord—the enemy might have a trap set for you today. Be deliberate in your praise. Watch what you say throughout the day. Ask God to bridle your tongue. Watch your step. Go only to those places God is leading you. Like most soldiers, you must learn to protect your feet. One wrong move and you could blow the mine. You can cause damage to yourself or those closest to you.

You don't have to be a general in the army to battle demonic spirits. Even the foot soldier sees some action. Have you run across any of these mines in your walk across the battlefield?

Lust (strong desire)

One of the most common spirits Christians will face is lust. It doesn't seem to matter if you live in a society where people are required to cover their entire bodies or a society where people are encouraged to show some skin, lust of the flesh will pay you a visit if you are in the Army of the Lord.

Even though we can lust after the flesh when things are going well in our lives, lust is usually used as a weapon by our enemy when we're feeling rejected or misunderstood by our loved ones. Suddenly, we'll have a strong need to feel wanted and desired, so we start our search. In some cases, Satan makes it real easy by placing someone in our lives at that very moment. A warning sign should go up when this happens. Some will stop and ask God to strengthen them. Others will jump right in and yield to sin.

Most people are aware of the phrase, "lust of the flesh," but you can lust after other things as well. Other lusts include a lust for food, alcohol and drugs. If you find yourself overconsuming these items, you have shifted Jesus' position in your life. Jesus is no longer in the center—something else is. How do you know when this happens? Let's see. Does any of this sound familiar in terms of your circumstances or someone you know?

When you feel happy about something, you celebrate by eating. When you feel sad, you respond by eating. Conclusion: food is the center of your life!

When you feel happy about something, you celebrate by drinking alcohol. When you feel sad, you respond by drinking alcohol. Conclusion: alcohol is the center of your life!

When you feel happy about something, you celebrate by taking a drug. When you feel sad, you respond by taking a drug. Conclusion: drugs are the center of your life!

Notice the difference here when Christ is the center. When you feel happy about something, you celebrate by praising the Lord. When you feel sad, you respond by praising the Lord. What will the world think whenever they see you? The Lord is the center of your life!

Greed (insatiable appetite)

In a highly competitive society it is hard to know where to draw the line in terms of success. For the Christian, all you need to remember is Christ is the center of your life. All of your other relationships should reflect this fact. When Christ is in the center, you will be less likely to find yourself competing for every possible advantage in the workplace or at school.

A hunger for more money shouldn't overtake you if you're paying your tithes and offerings. You are within

God's will for your finances so your economic life is paced by God's abundant blessings and not the stock market.

A hunger for power is tempered by knowing that Jesus rose with all power in His hands. Any power surge that you experience is a counterfeit—a temporary boost— nothing compared to God's power. Resist going after worldly power that is not sanctioned by God.

If God blesses you with material things like money and power, handle them like they are gifts from God. Use them for the glory of God. Never abuse your gifts. To whom much is given, much is required (Luke 12:48).

Envy (jealous)

This emotion occurs when Satan is trying to convince you there is some flaw in your character, physical body or material possessions. You start thinking about what you are missing in your life. You begin to compare yourself with others. Let us remind you that you are fearfully and wonderfully made (Psalm 139:14).

When you find yourself thinking someone is better (or better off) than you, turn that thing around on Satan. Remind him that the Scriptures say "there is no respect of persons with God" (Romans 2:11). Regardless of what the situation looks like on the outside, God is keeping track of your heart, your deeds and your faith. God looks on the inside. As long as you deny your carnal nature on a daily basis and follow God, you are in God's will (Luke 9:23).

As Christians, we are to seek understanding in all things (2 Timothy 2:7), especially when we find ourselves fighting these common spirits. For the Christian recruit, this is a momentous moment. You have made it far enough for Satan to notice your progress. He is now reaching down into his arsenal for his special weapons.

Take the time to talk to God. Let God know how you are interpreting these new events and then listen for God's explanation. You will learn that when you resist temptation, you become stronger in God! Your passions will be subdued. God will take over your mind and keep you focused on your goal of kingdom-building. You are well on your way to producing good fruit and recruiting others into the army. "But the fruit of the Spirit is love, joy, peace, longsuffering, gentleness, goodness, faith, meekness, temperance...And they that are Christ's have crucified the flesh with the affections and lusts. If we live in the Spirit, let us also walk in the Spirit. Let us not be desirous of vain glory, provoking one another, envying one another" (Galatians 5:22–24).

CHAPTER 5

THE FRONT LINES

*Greater love hath no man than this, that a man
lay down his life for his friends.*
—John 15:13

Did You Hear That? Clique

This part of your weaponry training is an interactive
exercise. By actually speaking along with the text, you
will be preparing your mind to avoid an alluring trap.
Somebody say, *cliques.*

Cliques are one of the most seductive traps on the
battlefield because it is a natural tendency for us to form
small groups. We gravitate towards other Christians. Even
in an army regiment, soldiers form close friendships with
particular individuals. Unfortunately, when those soldiers
are wounded and lost in battle, the morale of the squadron
decreases substantially. There have been many instances
of healthy soldiers losing their minds at the news of a
fallen comrade.

Forming friendships can be a healthy and natural human enterprise but the soldier in the Army of Christ must be wary of forming relationships that inhibit spiritual growth. Contact with other soldiers is a means to an end—not an end in and of itself. As a soldier you are expected to wear a breastplate of righteousness. In the natural realm, this part of the soldier's uniform helped to protect major internal body parts, including the heart. Protect your heart from relationships God has not approved. Somebody say, *cliques.*

Go with us, if you will, to the front lines of battle. Imagine yourself a part of an army regiment. You're traveling on foot across enemy territory. Oftentimes, the enemy will plant traps in the field of battle—amen? One of the most dangerous traps an enemy can set is a land mine.

Land mines can do a great deal of damage to the physical body. They can rip you apart. Similarly, the traps that the enemy sets for us in the spiritual realm can cause substantial damage to our spirit-man. These traps can also tear our lives apart. Right before a mine explodes, there is a clicking sound which signifies that the mine has been tripped. Somebody say, *click, click, click.*

Click, click, click

The next move is critical for the person standing on the mine. When we hear the word "clique" in the body of Christ, we have a problem. The reason cliques are a problem in the church body is because they represent division. A clique is a group of people who have set themselves apart from others: they only sit with each other in worship services; they only travel with certain other people; they have closed themselves off from ministering to others outside their circle. God has called each of us to minister to Him (Ezekiel 44:15–16) and those that He sends to us.

Clique

If you hear the word "clique" in your presence
    Know that the enemy has set a trap for you

If you ever hear a clique
    Stop and survey the field—look over your life
Perhaps the mine has been detonated already;
    perhaps it's a "dud"
Perhaps someone has already been over that
    territory
Your minister, perhaps, has taught you to look
    out for and avoid those cliques

If you think you are a part of a clique
    Slowly retreat from your position
Ask God to lift your foot from the dangerous
    spot you just stepped on
Ask God to redirect your steps
For the steps of a good man are ordered by God

Tell God that you heard a "click" and you realize
    that cliques are a trick of the enemy
Tell God you know that your next move can
    either maim you for life or kill your soul
    forever
Ask Him to neutralize the bomb
    For a clique can signify your demise

Tell God that you were just going along with the
    regiment
Attending service after service
Fighting battle after battle
Traveling with other soldiers you felt
    comfortable with
Rehashing old wartime stories
    Talking about the goodness of the Lord
Reminding your comrades to move carefully
    through the mine field
Explaining to them the lessons of spiritual
    warfare and how this equipment works
For you see, you've become the leader of your
    regiment

But before you knew it
    You heard a clique
Somebody say, *click, click, click.*

You weren't quite sure where the sound came from

Was it you or was it someone around you
Am I part of a clique?
Did anybody else hear that?

Sometimes the Holy Spirit will only speak to you
    about your situation
No one else will hear what He has to say to you

If you hear a clique, we recommend that you stop immediately. Fall on your knees and say, "Father, I stretch my hands to thee—no other help I know." Or sing the Psalm of David "God is our refuge and strength, a very present help in trouble" (Psalm 46:1).

For those of you who know something about battle, you know that land mines are usually set up right before the gold mine. In other words, the enemy is trying to stop you from reaching the prize that's on the other side. So, don't retreat when you come across a mine field—for your prize awaits you on the other side. Press forward with holy boldness. For the Bible says if you acknowledge the Lord in all your ways, He will direct your paths (Proverbs 3:6).

Thank God

Thank God for "mind"fields
Thank God for land mines

For without these tests, you could not grow
Without these traps, you could not prosper
Without these tricks from the enemy, you could
    not be promoted in the Army of the Lord.

Have you decided to follow Jesus?
For straight is the way and narrow the path
Your reward awaits you—on the other side

Do you want to see His face?
Do you want to bask in His presence?
Do you want to feel His love?
Do you want to see the other side—where your
    spirit will live forever?

Once you shed that old uniform and move up in
    the ranks of God's army
Earn a few stripes here and there

You can sit at the right hand of His throne
And have a little talk with Jesus

You can learn all the secrets of the universe
Or simply worship Him—just worship Him

Do you want to see Jesus?
Do you want to see Him?
If you want to see Him, say yes!

Thank God.

Waiting in the Trenches

Some soldiers will see battle early in their walk with Christ. Others may have to wait in the trenches for a while. Remember, God sent Moses to the backside of the dessert for forty years, tending somebody else's sheep, before He called him to the front lines of battle.

According to historians, trench warfare was used most often by American soldiers during World War I. Generals ordered their men to dig trenches that would provide protection from the advancing troops. Soldiers would write letters to their loved ones describing the trenches. Can you imagine life in the trenches? Apparently many things took place in the trenches—but most of the time was spent waiting.

"Wait on the LORD: be of good courage, and he shall strengthen thine heart: wait, I say, on the LORD" (Psalm 27:14). It's an odd feeling, waiting. Waiting for the next round of fire—the next round of attacks by the enemy. It can be an uneasy feeling. You're well dug into your position. You have a general idea of the direction of fire based on the last round of attack. In spiritual terms, you've had enough experience with the devil (demonic/evil forces) to recognize him. He tried to tempt you with money, sex, or power. You held on tight to your faith in God, resisted the devil, and he fled (James 4:7). So here you are, ready to make a move that will bring you closer in your relationship with God—ready to move forward.

But you're hesitant—you're waiting. Why? You know the devil is out there, setting another trap for you; so you spend your time in the trenches trying to figure out the next trap. What will it look like? Who will he send? What kind of weapons will he use?

Many Christians fail to realize that the anxiety they experience (anxiety attacks, panic disorders, phobias) in everyday life can be traced to some unforeseen and imagined danger. Mood disorders are so prevalent in society that they are often referred to as the common cold of mental disorders. People fear almost everything. The Christian is reminded that "God hath not given us the spirit of fear; but of power, and of love, and of a sound mind" (2 Timothy 1:7). Fear and anxiety are tricks of the enemy.

Instead of brooding about future traps or being fearful about what lies ahead, take this time to prepare your mind for the upcoming battles. Remember, this is spiritual warfare—not hand-to-hand combat. Not everyone will make it pass this stage. This is tough fighting. Will you make it? Are you committed? Are you prepared for battle?

If you are waiting in the trenches, use this time to prepare for your next season. Continue steadfast by:

1. Reading your Bible (get understanding through use of Bible aids)

2. Praying earnestly (find an ally or a prayer partner)

3. Fasting and seeking God's face

4. Praising & worshiping God

Remember, we serve the risen Savior. The war is over. We are simply fighting the battles to win more souls to Christ. Glory be to God, saints. Aren't you happy about it? Isn't that good news? Lift up your heads.

There are hurting, wounded people in the trenches. Instead of focusing on your situation at this time, reach out and help those around you. There may be some paralyzed soldiers in the trenches—people who have been hurt so badly that they cannot help themselves. They may be shattered and bruised. One of your duties as a soldier is to assist your comrades so the entire regiment can press forward. Know that God will never leave nor forsake you. He is down in the trenches with you—encouraging you every step of the way. God can heal and restore your spirit and your body while you're waiting in the trenches.

> There are hurting, wounded people in the trenches.

When Satan starts attacking your weakest points, just know your blessing is near. The enemy sends round after round of artillery fire when Christians draw near to victory. Learn to be uncomfortable until God blesses you.

The morale in the camp is high because we know we have the victory! Victories boost morale. Hallelujah. Let's continue our mission of kingdom-building! Let's move on to the next battle.

CHAPTER 6

ADVANCED WEAPONRY TRAINING

If my people, which are called by my name, shall
humble themselves, and pray, and seek my face,
and turn from their wicked ways; then will I hear
from heaven, and will forgive their sin and will
heal their land.

—2 Chronicles 7:14

Prayer

Hundreds of books are written about prayer every year. The focus is generally on how to pray, when to pray, what to pray, and why we should pray. Scientific studies show that the majority of people engage in some type of ritual activity they call prayer. However, most "prayers" do not include an attitude of submission to God. Many of us use prayer as an opportunity to ask God for material blessings (including happiness and good health) or ask His forgiveness for our sins.

We want to provide you, our now well-equipped soldier, with a piece of valuable information about prayer:

An essential element of prayer is *listening to God*. Prayer is a line of communication. While this may sound simple, most people do not approach prayer with the expectation that they might have to wait for God to respond to their needs, questions and/or desires.

Most of us talk, but we don't listen. Not only are we guilty of not taking time to listen to God, we want God to respond to our needs "right now."

Many countries are experiencing changes that lead to a fast-paced lifestyle. We have fast-food, quick-stop shopping, quick-pick lottery tickets, drive-thru banks and stop-and-drop dry cleaners that provide immediate services. It is not too surprising then, that we often find ourselves wanting a "right now" God. We say, "God please do this for me, right now. God, please fix this problem, right now. Please heal my body, right now."

Although God can do all things "right now," this type of approach puts us at a disadvantage and can hinder our relationship with God. God is likened to a magician rather than The Creator of the Universe. This undermines His authority in the minds of those who may be interested in becoming Christians. In fact, it makes Christians appear more like mystics than true believers. For example, if our prayers are not answered to our satisfaction then we say, "it must be God's will that we suffer through this situation." When our prayers are answered to our satisfaction, we will say "it must have been God's will. God worked it out." The problem with this mind set is it does not take into consideration God's Holy Word about His will. It also relieves us of all responsibility for our circumstances.

God's desire is spelled out in the covenant with our spiritual forefathers, Abraham, Isaac and Jacob. It is further described in the Ten Commandments of the Old Testament and throughout stories and parables in the New Testament. For example, God desires for us to be fruitful and multiply (Genesis1:28) and to be prosperous and healthy in mind, body and spirit (3 John 1:2). It is God's will that we love one another (John 13:34), that we live peaceably among one another if possible (Romans 12:18) and it is God's will that we live free from the bondage of sin (2 Peter 2:19–21). You will find it a lot easier to fight your spiritual battles if you have embraced your covenant relationship with God and established a clear line of communication.

When Moses went to the top of the mountain, he found himself in humble submission, waiting to receive God's Holy Word. While he stumbled at first to determine why he was drawn to the top of the mountain, he soon realized that all he needed to do was to be quiet and listen. Moses also came to understand that he did not have to rely on the promises made to his forefathers. God was making Himself available at that very moment to meet the needs of His people. When we seek the face of God, we are humbly and patiently waiting for God to speak to us—to speak to our personal situations. The Christian soldier must learn how to listen to the voice of God.

> The Christian soldier must learn how to listen to the voice of God.

We find ourselves confronted with some of the same problems as many individuals in the Bible. We are not sure what God has planned for our lives. Sometimes we are patient enough to wait. At other times, we take it upon ourselves to chart our destinies. God is seeking a people who understand the value and power of prayer. It is an awesome weapon. But like any weapon in an arsenal, its purpose must be clearly understood. We must know why prayer works.

I Know Prayer Works ... but Why?

Even though God bestows upon us His mercy and grace on a daily basis, an answered prayer is usually a response on God's part to fulfilling His end of the bargain. Remember, God said, "If my people ... shall humble themselves ... pray ... seek ... turn ... then will I ... forgive ... heal." (2 Chronicles 7:14). This is an example of a covenant—an agreement made between God and man. If you do this, then I'll do that.

It is exciting to know that God will not leave or forsake us. It is exciting to know that God will answer our prayers. It is exciting to know that God never desires death and destruction to the spirit. It is exciting to know that God is always available to listen and advise. Now, if we can just get ourselves to the place where we are ready and willing to wait to hear from God—oh, what an awesome moment that would be.

For those of you who have experienced the voice of God and the move of the Holy Spirit, you know without a doubt that God is real! He is an awesome God! It is our prayer that every Christian will have a personal experience with God. It is through prayer that you can establish this intimate relationship. God is merciful and will not forget the covenant.

The commandments given to Moses outline aspects of our relationship with God and our relationship with others. In any relationship, the parties must come to an agreement on the goals and duties of each party. Clear communication is the only way to achieve this goal. You must not only tell the person what you need or desire but listen to what the other party needs and/or desires. This is the only way both parties will be satisfied, fulfilled and happy with the relationship. When you are satisfied with a relationship, you are willing to make sacrifices for the other person. So it is with God. Once you agree to become a true disciple, you come into covenant agreement with God. You will have to make sacrifices along the way.

A poignant example of the importance of establishing a personal relationship with God was provided by the senior ministry of Wake Chapel Church. They decided to put on a play that featured various church members approaching the gates of heaven, meeting a stranger and discussing why they were certain they would be able to open these gates and enter heaven (Revelation 21:12–27).

The characters in the play focused on four themes. Some characters believed they would enter heaven because of who they knew in the church, for example, being best friends with the senior minister. Other characters insisted they would be allowed to enter the gates because of their extended years of church service. Another group emphasized the type of service they provided to the church body, such as praise and worship team leaders. Then others simply thought abiding by certain commandments would grant them entrance, especially occasionally paying tithes.

None of the church members were able to open the gates to the city. They all walked away disappointed and disgruntled, not really understanding what went wrong. Even the minister was turned down by St. Peter. The last scene of this dramatic production featured the minister explaining to his church members why all of them (including himself) were denied entrance into heaven. He explained that many of them did not study the Bible, follow God's commandments, or listen to God's instructions for their lives.

Once we sign up for active duty in the Army of Jesus Christ, we are responsible for developing a personal relationship with God. It is through prayer that God gives us our "orders." We are led by the Holy Spirit to join a certain church. We are taken through boot camp to learn how to be an effective soldier. We are dispatched to different areas of the country to spread the good news of our risen Savior (perhaps not those areas we find the most desirable nor to the people we feel the most comfortable around).

It is through continual prayer that God renews our strength! It is through continual prayer that God assures us He is on our side—because the battle is the Lord's, we are assured of victory. We are the winners. We will be victorious. Hallelujah! Praises be to God Almighty!

Why Is Listening Important?

What soldier would not listen to a war veteran, the very person who has seen combat and knows the enemy? God knows everything. He is the creator of the universe. He knows your enemy and He knows your strengths and weaknesses. God was around when Satan tempted Adam and Eve in the garden. God was around when Satan tempted His son, Jesus Christ. God witnessed all of the battles (physical and spiritual) fought by mankind since the beginning of time.

God can prepare you physically, mentally, and spiritually for your upcoming battles. It is through prayer that you come to know what God has planned for your life. Listening to those plans will help you avoid traps set by the enemy. Listening to God will propel you forward on this walk of faith. It will prepare you to witness to others. Listening to God will help you avoid the three "mis's" of prayer.

Three Mis's

We misuse prayer. A frequently cited scripture is, "Ask and it shall be given unto you" (Matthew 7:7). Some people end that scripture right there without considering seeking, finding and knocking. We abuse our privileges with God by treating Him like a spiritual Santa Claus. We must seek God as a spiritual experience and know that we can't always get what we want. God's omnipresence does not mean that God is at our disposal.

We misunderstand prayer. Again, prayer is the venue through which we establish our covenant relationship with God. Prayer is not optional for the Christian. It is a necessary part of our relationship with God. Either we talk to God or there is no relationship. This should sound familiar. Human relationships are founded on the same principle. Communication is essential to the maintenance of a relationship.

We mismanage prayer. We only think to pray in times of distress. Political leaders call for global prayer and families often come together to pray when they are dealing with tragedy and grief. For the Christian soldier, prayer must be consistent, intentional and deliberate. Intentional prayer seeks out what God's will is for our lives. It is not just praying for stuff. Prayer positions us to receive the power of the Holy Spirit.

> Prayer positions us to receive the power of the Holy Spirit.

Prayer Warriors

The power of prayer is evident in the lives of Christians who have made it a part of their daily routines. When our leaders instruct us to pray, prayer warriors do not restrict their prayers to asking God to "heal the sick, provide peace to those nations in turmoil…do this, do that." Instead, prayer warriors thank God for His mercy, grace, peace, love and longsuffering. Prayer warriors thank God for His Holy Spirit. Prayer warriors thank God for the death, burial and resurrection of His Son Jesus. Prayer warriors praise God, for He is worthy of all the praises, glory and honor! Prayer warriors magnify the Lord; they exalt Him and lift His name on High! Does this sound familiar? Are you a prayer warrior? Hallelujah! Glory to God!

Prayer is essential for communicating with God as well as promoting well-being in your spirit. When you are in touch with God, you are not easily distressed by every personal tragedy. As you grow in Christ, you will come to recognize God as Jehovah Jirah (your provider), Jehovah Shalom (He gives you peace), Jehovah Shammah (He is there with you) and Jehovah Nissi (He is your refuge and you should rally around God as the leader of the battle).

As a Christian soldier, you must come to a place in God where you feel assured that God is in control. Once you reach a certain spiritual level in God, you will recognize spiritual warfare. You will not be intimidated by spiritual battles. You will be a ready soldier.

Some Christians are overly concerned with the things of the world and do not pay enough attention to the spiritual battles that slow them down. Once you establish a consistent prayer life, it will become easier to stay focused on God's kingdom. God takes care of His

> Some Christians are overly concerned with
> the things of the world and
> do not pay enough attention to
> the spiritual battles that slow them down.

children and He will reveal Himself to you by answering your prayers. Prayer will allow you to have a meaningful relationship with God.

Prayer is a viable mainstay in your spiritual diet. Various scriptures emphasize the importance of a prayer life among God's chosen people. The Scriptures provide many examples where God's people recognized His voice and then applied what He told them to do. For example, Elijah recognized the difference between noise and the still, small voice of God (1 Kings 19:11–13).

Prayer is an effective coping strategy that will help you deal with the spiritual and worldly battles of your everyday life. Prayer involves contemplation, meditation and activation. You can see in the Scriptures that Jesus prayed as part of his daily routine. Jesus told Peter that His prayer was that Peter's faith fail him not. If you don't pray, then your faith will fail. In order for your faith to be active, you must pray.

The Prayer of Faith

The prayer of faith is of critical importance to the Christian (James 5:13–16). Prayer is not just asking, but believing. There is no need to pray unless you believe that your prayer will be answered. Prayer, like praise and worship, is another method of invoking God's power and commanding God's authority. The Bible tells us through scriptures that we should always pray (Luke 18:1; 1 Thessalonians 5:17).

Prayer is used by many people to ask God for a physical healing of the body. If you are feeling pressed, oppressed or experiencing some type of traumatic experience, then you should pray about those particular circumstances. God does not specify as to the severity of problems. If you are feeling distressed at any level, you should pray. We know that God can heal all types of sickness and disease (Matthew 4:23; 17:15–18).

As a soldier in the Army of the Lord, you must never forget to acknowledge the source of your healing. Many people fall back on prayer when things are not going well in their lives. As soon as the situation changes for the better, everyone is acknowledged and praised except God. As a Christian, you must know for certain that God is the head of your life and all things work together for good to them that love God (Romans 8:28).

Although there are many examples of physical healing in the Scriptures, the Bible speaks repeatedly of spiritual healing. Healing refers to more than the absence of sickness in the body. God desires for His children to have "wholistic" healing. Many soldiers in the Army of the Lord miss this point! We often equate sickness with physical illness. We ask you today, is your goal healing or to be made whole?

Whole means all of you. Your healing will include a healing of the soul. Remember, the prayer of faith shall save the sick, not heal the sick. Save the sick is an in-depth healing that addresses all manners of maladies in your soul and spirit. You can be physically well but mentally disturbed. Amen?

Ultimately, a complete healing has to come from God. An example of a "wholistic" healing was shared with us by someone who acknowledged his hope in Christ and simultaneously stopped smoking, drinking and doing drugs without experiencing any withdrawal symptoms! When you witness a "wholistic" healing, you should feel led to worship the Almighty God. Hallelujah!

Have you ever considered how Jesus handled the situation with the ten lepers (Luke 17:12)? All of the lepers were healed, but only one was made whole. This particular man acknowledged the source of his healing before going to show himself to others. Jesus said, "Thy faith made thee whole." He experienced both a physical healing and a spiritual healing. Once you are healed "wholistically" it doesn't really matter if your physical body is ever diseased again. Your mind has been prepared for the kingdom of God.

If you are depressed, lonely, lack energy and enthusiasm or just want to be made whole, take a minute to pray this specific prayer of faith with us:

Reveal yourself to me, Lord.

Give me the strength to go where
you would have me to go.

Give me the courage to witness to those
you bring to my attention.

Lord, empower me so I can empower others.

Lift my spirits, so I can lift others.

Let your light shine in me so others
may be drawn to your kingdom.

Heal my mind, body and soul. Make me whole. Amen.

Once you learn to listen for God's instructions, then you can use prayer as a weapon against evil forces. The children of Israel often became impatient when faced with the possibility that they would be doing battle with their enemies. They wanted God to come "right now" and rescue them. Their disobedience and thirst for a "right now" God delayed their blessings for forty years.

Without prayer, you are a wandering recruit. You might have good intentions. You might volunteer in organizations that help take care of the sick, feed the hungry and clothe the naked, but without the blessings of God, your works are in vain. They do not help build the kingdom of God. You are simply being a good citizen. Ask God what it is He would have you to do. Make your works count. Get in touch with the Creator. Talk to God. Listen for His response. Go pray!

John tells us that God is a spirit and those that worship Him must worship him in spirit and in truth (John 4:24). If we are humans and God is spirit, then we must become spiritual beings to communicate with God. Our desires are then turned towards God and not ourselves. "But seek ye first the kingdom of God, and his righteousness; and all these things shall be added unto you" (Matthew 6:33). We must all pray that our lives are prioritized correctly so God can get the glory out of all we say and do.

When you read the Bible, how do you know it applies to you? You must know through prayer. You should be prayerfully reading, prayerfully considering things and prayerfully contemplating things. It's not just thinking positive thoughts but your thoughts should be guided by the parameters of prayer. Ask God, "Lord, what would you have me to do; what would you have me to say; how would you have me to react to this situation? Help me to have the right spirit, to have the right frame of mind, to do justice, to walk humbly before you." Prayer becomes the umbrella under which we direct our lives because we want to please God.

A key role model for prayer was Jesus. Jesus lived a prayerful life. The old prophets also constantly prayed to God that they would have the strength to do God's work. It is no different today. We are very technologically proficient and very sophisticated in all that we do, but it is good, old fashioned prayer that is going to keep us focused in times like these.

Prayer is an essential part of your daily walk through life. Just as you experience various developmental stages of life, so you mature in your prayer life. Once you have been renewed and transformed in your mind, then God will reveal His perfect will for your life. You will come to understand that church is necessary, church worship is empowering and prayer helps you to deal with problem areas. You will learn that there are some things over which you have no control, but through prayer you are able to cope with adversity. Under the auspices of prayer, you can receive all you need and become all you have the potential to become. Listening, listening, listening.

> Prayer is an essential part of your daily walk through life.

As children, we were taught to listen to our parents, teachers and those in authority over us. In order to complete a homework assignment, for example, we had to have a clear understanding of what the teacher instructed us to do. Similarly, when we read the Word of God, the only way we are able to keep the Word is by faith and through prayer. Prayer allows us to communicate with God, hear from God, and then listen to God.

We must continue to pray that the obstacles and stumbling blocks we face be removed. Man ought always to pray and not faint (Luke 18:1). We must pray for character—those aspects of our personality that infringe upon our ability to win the battles. Prayer helps us to see what is godly and what is not godly about us. We are at war. We may not win every battle in the war, but we want to win enough to make a difference.

Prayer is both vertical and horizontal. It is vertical in terms of praying to the Almighty God, giving reverence and honor to the King. Prayer is horizontal in terms of praying for others. In order to maintain our relationship with God and others we must include forgiveness in our prayers. Unless we can forgive each other we cannot expect to be forgiven by God. We are to make all requests known to God. If you visualize this type of prayer life, you have formed a cross. In order to complete the covenant promise, you must have a good relationship with God and others through His Son Jesus who died on the cross.

The onus is on us to listen to God—to listen to what He says. Some things are too difficult to deal with so we must constantly seek a prayerful mind, spirit and heart. God spoke to John throughout the book of Revelation regarding the churches. A common phrase was, "He that hath an ear, let him hear what the Spirit saith unto the churches." As you spend time in your church home, learn how to listen to the voice of God!

It is through prayer that we come to know what God has planned for our lives. God doesn't always use noise and clamor, but often comes in the stillness. This is why it is important to have that quiet place where God can speak to you. Although you may feel that you are not important in the larger scheme of God's universe, there is

a place for you in God's ultimate plan. Prayer will reveal
this to you. Imagine the following conversation with God.

A Conversation with God

I saw a sky full of stars,
And I started to cry
I cried, because there were so many stars
It would be so easy to get lost

So one day I asked God,
  With all of those stars in the hemisphere
  How do you know them?

He said,
  There you are
  Your relation to the other stars in the universe is
    what makes you unique
  You are unique
  Without you there, in that place, the universe is
    not what I made it

He went on to say,
  I do know you
  I made you

I cried some more, because I had to tell Him
  But I denied you
  I went around you

He said,
  I know
  But I never let you leave my universe
  You were still there

Still in place
My tears kept flowing.

He said,
Now let me show you what I have in store for
you,
Where I want you to shine in other peoples'
lives

And then I saw
I was flooded with a sense of peace

And God said,
Now that you know your place in my universe,
Shine.

It is so important for you to know where you fit in the universe. God's creation had a purpose and meaning. You are a part of that creation, therefore your life has purpose and meaning. You are not a random occurrence or a mistake. God knew you would be born and He desires to have a personal relationship with you. It is your choice, as it has always been. Will you choose God?

You must seek God's council while He is near (Isaiah 55:6). You might say, "Why should I talk to God?" The answer is simple—because God cares. God cares about the way you feel. God cares about your current circumstances. God cares about your future. You will never be able to fully understand why God loves you so much (Isaiah 55:6–9), but we can assure you that He does. His mercy and grace are everlasting.

CHAPTER 7

BECOMING A CHRISTIAN

CHRISTIANITY AS A PROCESS

*Though I speak with the tongues of men and of
angels, and have not charity, I am become as
sounding brass, or a tinkling cymbal. And though
I have the gift of prophecy, and understand all
mysteries, and all knowledge; and though I have
all faith, so that I could remove mountains, and
have not charity, I am nothing. And though I
bestow all my goods to feed the poor, and though
I give my body to be burned, and have not
charity, it profiteth me nothing.*
—1 Corinthians 13:1–3

Questions about the Process

How do you know if you are a Christian?

The first clue to being a Christian is to know that you
have been changed and secondly, you have the ability to
accept people as they are. If you meet someone who is
living contrary to God's Holy Word, you should pray for

their conversion. You will notice in many Bible stories that Jesus had few difficulties with sinners. It was usually the people in organized religion who challenged Jesus' authority and ways. The scribes continually hounded him and tried to cajole him to blend in with them. It is no different today.

Being a Christian is a spiritual experience that has physical manifestations, not the other way around. A Christian looks like everybody else, however, the Christian's thought processes should reflect the mind of Christ. That is why the attack of the enemy is so vehement. Jesus indicates that love is the determining factor as to the proof of one's discipleship. God is loving and compassionate.

> Being a Christian is a spiritual experience that has physical manifestations, not the other way around.

Does the way I dress determine my Christian status?

Simply stated, actions always speak louder than words or looks. There are, however, some denominations whose foundation for Christendom is based on appearance more than anything else. You must be careful not to sway to either extreme. On the one hand, dressing conservative for the sake of tradition can border on self-righteous fanaticism. On the other hand, it is not likely that you will be successful in convincing the sinner that you are somehow different from those in the world if your style of dress is defined in a negative way by those in the world.

You must ask God to reveal His will and way in your life. Once your heart has been transformed, your actions will fall in line with God's will. You don't earn God's favor by being a conformist. Instead, you must put yourself in a position to respond to God's Holy Spirit.

How long does it take to become a Christian?

Becoming a Christian is a life long process. In any process, the most important factor is time. In the case of Christianity, the key area of transformation is the mind—this is what can take so long. The individual is transformed by the renewing of the mind, according to Romans, chapter 12. At each step of success in Christ, you get closer and closer to God—you become more Christlike.

Think about climbing a ladder. As you persevere in trials and tribulations and sow good fruit in the kingdom of God, you move higher and higher up the ladder. Slothfulness and inactivity as a soldier will maintain your current placement on the ladder. You neither move backward nor forward. Time is passing you by, you are not fulfilling your purpose and your blessings are on hold.

Sinful acts can take you backwards on the ladder. Again, you lose precious time when you fall for the tricks of the enemy. Remember, the measuring stick is the life of Christ. What distinguishes the Christian from the non-Christian is the ability and willingness to get up and try again. A key point here is to develop a relationship with God and come to understand His expectations for your life.

Isn't my faith in God and Christ enough to make me a Christian?

Without faith it is impossible to please God (Hebrews 11:6), but love is the catalyst for it all. If you come to God you must believe that He is and that He rewards those who seek him with diligence. When you love God, you develop a compassion for people. The Bible tells us that faith without works is dead (James 2:17). Don't get lulled into being idle. Slothfulness, or laziness, is a sin.

Isn't confessing with my mouth and believing in my heart that Jesus is Lord, the only thing I really have to do to be a Christian?

This scripture is actually indicative of the process of becoming more like Christ. The Greek translation of the word confess means "to acknowledge that you are in agreement; a deep conviction." The Christian moves into (or towards) salvation after hearing God's Holy Word and developing a strong belief in Jesus. As suggested by different characters in the Bible, anyone can confess a belief in Jesus Christ. Even Satan acknowledged that Jesus was the Son of God.

The Greek translation of the word believe, pisteuo, means "to entrust or have faith in." In general, salvation is a process. Your mind has to be changed. The story of Paul's walk on the road to Damascus is an excellent example of someone who believed after being persuaded to change his perspective and follow God.

When should I start inviting others to my church to learn about Christ?

You should always feel comfortable inviting others to church, but avoid trying to entice individuals to leave their current church. Those who believe in manipulating others into attending their church are on the wrong track. This practice is tactless, disgraceful, unethical, immoral, self-serving, ungodly and unholy. God says He draws us with loving-kindness, not by schemes and craftiness.

The correct term is evangelization for the purpose of soul-winning. When you are ready for evangelizing, God will place people in your life to whom He expects you to minister. You want to be ready when that time comes. To prepare yourself for those individuals, pray daily, read your Bible on a consistent basis and attend church services (Sunday school, Bible study, evangelizing classes or conferences).

The Anointing

In the Old Testament, the anointing was always used to represent a consecration for service. It usually refers to anointing with oil. The oil is symbolic of God's spirit. The anointing also has the same basic connotation in the New Testament. However, in the New Testament, oil represents the Holy Spirit. The anointing is indicative of God's certification upon one's life for service in kingdom building.

In other words, the anointing is the power of God. It is not to be taken lightly. It is not to be spoken of lightly. The anointing refers to the physical manifestation of being touched by God. Most Christians recognize God's anointing. It is more difficult to explain than to feel, but we will give it a try.

Most people recognize God's anointing when it is evidenced through speech—singing or speaking. Singers can have their tongues anointed and the lyrics they utter will touch the heart and soul. Preachers can have an anointed tongue and the preached word will go forth and speak directly to personal situations. Unlike a soothsayer, however, the anointed word will both speak to you and give you the answer to your problems. Of course, God works through all human abilities and talents. Musicians can play instruments under the anointing. People can mime under the anointing.

Those in the body of Christ can be under the anointing at any time. When the anointing is high, it can fall on an unsuspecting bystander. Some people who have been under the anointing cry for no apparent reason. Perhaps they are feeling the compassion of Jesus. Some begin to sing songs they never rehearsed. They were simply moved to sing that song. Others dance like David danced (2 Samuel 6:14).

It is the anointing that gives you the words to say to strangers—the exact words that will convince them to turn their lives over to God. Remember, it's not you—it is the anointing. The anointing is the power of God. The anointing puts fire in your evangelizing efforts.

> The anointing puts fire
> in your evangelizing efforts.

Because man is born of flesh, he can use or misuse his anointing. God grants man favor when He gives him His anointing. Those who are repeat offenders in sinful acts have set aside the power of the anointing. Suddenly the songs don't seem to move the audience—the preached word becomes harder to convey—witnessing to others seems burdensome. You no longer command the crowds, receive invitations, peak interests or have influence with others. You have somehow abused God's favor.

Some people say you can lose your anointing. What generally happens is that when we sin, we are out of the will of God. Being out of the will of God means we are no longer in sync or attuned to God's voice. We sing, preach, and speak but it doesn't have the same effect on others that it once had. God is no longer leading the way into spiritual battle. We are uncovered. We are open prey to the sins of the world and the temptations of the devil when we're not walking in our anointing. That is why it is so important to try not to sin and when we act against the will of God, go before Him sorrowful and full of repentance, begging His forgiveness. We can do all things, but only through Christ Jesus who gives us the strength.

There are many instances in the Bible where God withdrew His Holy Spirit. For example, Saul lost favor with God when he listened to the voices of the people instead of seeking God's advice and following God's counsel (1 Samuel 15:24). What is most troubling about Saul's story is the impact a leader's decisions can have on the church body. Blatant and wanton acts affect the souls of others. Saul listened to the people and this caused the entire nation to be in an uproar.

The anointing can also be described as the positive intrusion of God's Spirit into a person's life. The Apostle Paul's life demonstrates this phenomenon. Originally, Paul punished and killed the Christians until that day on the road to Damascus. Paul was blinded by a light for three days. In fact, he had to be led around before he regained his sight. From that point on, Paul was a positive force for Christianity.

In essence, the entire purpose of spiritual warfare from Satan's point of view is to get you out of good standing with God—to compromise your integrity with God. Once you become a soldier and come to understand and use your special gifts for the building up of God's kingdom, Satan will try to sift you as wheat (Luke 22:31).

You must stay alert. Be mindful and always pray that the Holy Spirit leads and guides you through this faith walk. Be mindful of your flesh, your spirit and your mind— each should be fed a balanced diet.

Prepared for Battle

Now, you are prepared for battle! You are ready to face the challenges of everyday life. Allow us to summarize the secrets to successful spiritual warfare.

1. *Surrender* your heart, mind and soul to God. Once you confess with your mouth and believe in your heart that Jesus is Lord, you are qualified to wear the armor of God. You are a recruit in the Army of the Lord. Congratulations!

2. You have found a church home that will serve as your home base for *boot camp*. Your spiritual growth now begins. A number of events and situations will occur in your life that can cause retreat or advance in your growth in Christ. Let your church home serve as both a testing ground and a filling station (where you can get rejuvenated to go back on the front lines to face the attack of the enemy). Listen to your drill instructors and follow the leader.

3. Now it is time to go off to *battle*. A critical piece of equipment is your helmet. You must protect your mind. Satan will play tricks on you and set a variety of traps in the "mind fields." Be patient and wait on the Lord. God will strengthen your heart. Remember your mission training.

4. At some point you will need to consider using some *advanced weaponry*. You can't always battle the enemy on your own. You may need

intercessory prayer, so be prepared to ask others to intercede on your behalf. Ask your squad mates (or fellow recruits) to pray for your situation; this is especially important when you are seeking the healing power of our Lord and Savior, Jesus Christ.

The good news of Jesus Christ is that you are no longer bound by your humanity. You can defeat the enemy who comes to conquer your soul. You can do all things through Christ and that includes binding up the demons in your life. Under the New Covenant of Christ, you can develop a personal relationship with God. You can come to know God through the Scriptures. You will find God's grace is sufficient and His mercy endures forever. This is good news. You will find that conforming to the law does not guarantee salvation but salvation is a gift from God. Yield yourself to God and your mind will be transformed so that conforming to His will and way will be easy. Soon you will notice your life is in line with God's will.

Becoming a Christian is a lifelong process but it is the anointing that guides the Christian through this faith walk. You cannot bear the fruit of the spirit (love, joy, peace) without the anointing or God's Holy Spirit. As a Christian, you have access to the power of the Holy Spirit. Use your power. Use your gifts. God has equipped you with all of the armor and weaponry you will need to be a successful and prosperous soldier. Remember, God is in control. As long as you stay connected to God through prayer, you are a winner. Take back what the devil stole from you. Be encouraged! Be blessed! Welcome to the Army of the Lord!

ABOUT THE AUTHORS

Pamela Braboy Jackson resides in Bloomington, Indiana with her husband Paul and stepson David. Pamela graduated from Indiana University in 1993 with a Ph.D. in Sociology. After graduation, she worked for seven years at Duke University in Durham, North Carolina. It was during her time in North Carolina that she renewed her faith in Christ and joined Wake Chapel Church in Raleigh. There she served on the Youth for Christ Ministry as a youth advisor; chair of the Health Care Advocacy Ministry; and armour-bearer to the pastor's wife, Cheryl. Each of these activities brought Pamela closer to Christ as she found herself serving as a prayer intercessor for the continued strength of others who were under spiritual attack.

In 2001 she began working for Indiana University as an associate professor. Since moving to Bloomington, Pamela has joined Sherwood Oaks Christian Church where she is currently serving on the Women's Ministry, Missions Ministry and Disaster Relief Team. She spends her free time with family, volunteering in the community at a youth club and playing softball, where she's best known as "Positive Pam," the cheerleader.

Pamela continues to publish in mainstream areas of medical sociology, focusing on self-esteem, work and family stress, and adolescent mental health. She has given public addresses and motivational speeches to school and work groups. Some of her early research on women's health has been cited in Glamour Magazine.

Pamela has learned through trusting in God, believing in God's Holy Word, and witnessing His miraculous powers that spiritual things cannot be understood by a carnal mind.

J. J. Wilkins, Jr. is the Senior Pastor of Wake Chapel Church, located in Raleigh, North Carolina. Pastor Wilkins is a noted speaker and teacher and has received numerous awards for his outstanding commitment to community service. He is married to Cheryl Renee and they are the proud parents of two sons, John Jasper III and Jared Carlton.

Pastor Wilkins has served on several boards and associations on a local and national level, and is often featured in the media as a goodwill ambassador and community spokesman. Pastor Wilkins graduated from New Hampshire College, attended Yale Divinity School and received a Masters of Divinity degree from Duke University.

He received the "Pastor of the Year" award at the 16th Annual Waljo People's Choice Awards in March of 2001. He also serves on the Yale University Alumni Schools Committee, the advisory panel for the Z. Smith Reynolds Foundation and as a board member for the National Collegiate Music Conference and the National Baptist Housing Commission.

"*Preparing for Battle* is a loud wake up call to young Christians and mature Christians who have become complacent. I like the book because it screams to the reader, "Wake up! WE are at WAR!" The authors present the reality of Christian life, that we are in a daily war against Satan and the forces of evil in this world. But instead of being a depressing or fearful situation the authors focus on the fact that the Lord Jesus has assured His people that He and those who obey Him have won the war (Romans 8:37)."

"Furthermore, through the Word of God, hymns, poems and sound spiritual admonitions, the authors practically show how God has equipped us for victory for our daily battles and the war. Because the book is short and concisely written it is a very practical book for fighting the spiritual battle."

—Art Belcher
Member, University Bible Fellowship

The Big Red Bible
45.00

II Thess
2 3-6-1

1-800-622-2767
Rev 19:1